CANDIDA

1894-5

Candida.   A Mystery.
By Bernard Shaw.

Constable and Company
Ltd. London: 1929.

Printed in Great Britain by R. & R. CLARK, LIMITED, *Edinburgh.*

CANDIDA

ACT I

*A fine October morning in the north east quarter of London,
a vast district miles away from the London of Mayfair and
St James's, and much less narrow, squalid, fetid and airless
in its slums. It is strong in unfashionable middle class life;
wide-streeted; myriad-populated; well served with ugly iron
urinals, Radical clubs, and tram lines carrying a perpetual
stream of yellow cars; enjoying in its main thoroughfares the
luxury of grass-grown "front gardens" untrodden by the foot
of man save as to the path from the gate to the hall door;
blighted by a callously endured monotony of miles and miles of
unlovely brick houses, black iron railings, stony pavements,
slated roofs, and respectably ill dressed or disreputably poorly
dressed people, quite accustomed to the place, and mostly plodding
uninterestedly about somebody else's work. The little energy and
eagerness that crop up shew themselves in cockney cupidity and
business "push." Even the policemen and the chapels are not
infrequent enough to break the monotony. The sun is shining
cheerfully; there is no fog; and though the smoke effectually
prevents anything, whether faces and hands or bricks and mortar,
from looking fresh and clean, it is not hanging heavily enough
to trouble a Londoner.*

This desert of unattractiveness has its oasis. Near the

outer end of the Hackney Road is a park of 217 acres, fenced in, not by railings, but by a wooden paling, and containing plenty of greensward, trees, a lake for bathers, flower beds which are triumphs of the admired cockney art of carpet gardening, and a sandpit, originally imported from the sea-side for the delight of children, but speedily deserted on its becoming a natural vermin preserve for all the petty fauna of Kingsland, Hackney and Hoxton. A bandstand, an un-furnished forum for religious, anti-religious and political orators, cricket pitches, a gymnasium, and an old fashioned stone kiosk are among its attractions. Wherever the prospect is bounded by trees or rising green grounds, it is a pleasant place. Where the ground stretches flat to the grey palings, with bricks and mortar, sky signs, crowded chimneys and smoke beyond, the prospect (in 1894) makes it desolate and sordid.

The best view of Victoria Park is commanded by the front window of St Dominic's Parsonage, from which not a brick is visible. The parsonage is semi-detached, with a front garden and a porch. Visitors go up the flight of steps to the porch: tradespeople and members of the family go down by a door under the steps to the basement, with a breakfast room, used for all meals, in front, and the kitchen at the back. Up-stairs, on the level of the hall door, is the drawing room, with its large plate glass window looking out on the park. In this, the only sitting room that can be spared from the children and the family meals, the parson, the Reverend James Mavor Morell, does his work. He is sitting in a strong round backed revolving chair at the end of a long table, which stands across the window, so that he can cheer himself with a view of the park over his left shoulder. At the opposite end of the table, adjoining it, is a little table only half as wide as the other, with a typewriter on it. His typist is sitting at this machine, with her back to the window. The large table is littered with pamphlets, journals, letters, nests of drawers, an office diary, postage scales and the like. A spare chair for visitors having business with the parson is in the middle, turned to his end. Within reach of his hand is a stationery case, and a photograph *in a frame. The wall behind him is fitted with bookshelves, on which an adept eye can measure the parson's casuistry and divinity by Maurice's Theological Essays and a complete set of Browning's poems, and the reformer's politics by a yellow backed Progress and Poverty, Fabian Essays, A Dream of John Ball, Marx's Capital, and half a dozen other literary landmarks in Socialism. Facing him on the other side of the room, near the typewriter, is the door. Further down, opposite the fireplace, a bookcase stands on a cellaret, with a sofa near it. There is a generous fire burning; and the hearth, with a comfortable arm-chair and a black japanned flower-painted coal scuttle at one side, a miniature chair for a boy or girl on the other, a varnished wooden mantelpiece, with neatly moulded shelves, tiny bits of mirror let into the panels, a travelling clock in a leather case (the inevitable wedding present), and on the wall above a large autotype of the chief figure in Titian's Assumption of the Virgin, is very inviting. Altogether the room is the room of a good housekeeper, vanquished, as far as the table is concerned, by an untidy man, but elsewhere mistress of the situation. The furniture, in its ornamental aspect, betrays the style of the advertized " drawing-room suite " of the pushing suburban furniture dealer; but there is nothing useless or pretentious in the room. The paper and panelling are dark, throwing the big cheery window and the park outside into strong relief.*

The Reverend James Mavor Morell is a Christian Social-ist clergyman of the Church of England, and an active member of the Guild of St Matthew and the Christian Social Union. A vigorous, genial, popular man of forty, robust and goodlook-ing, full of energy, with pleasant, hearty, considerate manners, and a sound unaffected voice, which he uses with the clean athletic articulation of a practised orator, and with a wide range and perfect command of expression. He is a first rate clergyman, able to say what he likes to whom he likes, to lecture people without setting himself up against them, to impose his authority on them without humiliating them, and, on occasion, to interfere in their business without impertinence. His well-spring of enthusiasm and sympathetic emotion has never run dry

*for a moment: he still eats and sleeps heartily enough to win
the daily battle between exhaustion and recuperation triumphantly. Withal, a great baby, pardonably vain of his powers
and unconsciously pleased with himself. He has a healthy com-
plexion; a good forehead, with the brows somewhat blunt, and
the eyes bright and eager; a mouth resolute, but not particularly
well cut; and a substantial nose, with the mobile, spreading
nostrils of the dramatic orator, void, like all his features, of
subtlety.*

*The typist, Miss Proserpine Garnett, is a brisk little woman
of about* 30, *of the lower middle class, neatly but cheaply
dressed in a black merino skirt and a blouse, rather pert and
quick of speech, and not very civil in her manner, but sensitive
and affectionate. She is clattering away busily at her machine
whilst Morell opens the last of his morning's letters. He
realizes its contents with a comic groan of despair.*

PROSERPINE. Another lecture?

MORELL. Yes. The Hoxton Freedom Group want me
to address them on Sunday morning [*he lays great emphasis
on " Sunday," this being the unreasonable part of the business*].
What are they?

PROSERPINE. Communist Anarchists, I think.

MORELL. Just like Anarchists not to know that they
cant have a parson on Sunday! Tell them to come
to church if they want to hear me : it will do them good.
Say I can only come on Mondays and Thursdays. Have
you the diary there?

PROSERPINE [*taking up the diary*] Yes.

MORELL. Have I any lecture on for next Monday?

PROSERPINE [*referring to diary*] Tower Hamlets Radical
Club.

MORELL. Well, Thursday then?

PROSERPINE. English Land Restoration League.

MORELL. What next?

PROSERPINE. Guild of St Matthew on Monday. In-
dependent Labor Party, Greenwich Branch, on Thursday.

Monday, Social-Democratic Federation, Mile End Branch. Thursday, first Confirmation class— [*Impatiently*] Oh, I'd better tell them you cant come. Theyre only half a dozen ignorant and conceited costermongers without five shillings between them.

MORELL [*amused*] Ah ; but you see theyre near relatives of mine, Miss Garnett.

PROSERPINE [*staring at him*] Relatives of yours!

MORELL. Yes : we have the same father — in Heaven.

PROSERPINE [*relieved*] Oh, is that all ?

MORELL [*with a sadness which is a luxury to a man whose voice expresses it so finely*] Ah, you dont believe it. Everybody says it : nobody believes it — nobody. [*Briskly, getting back to business*] Well, well ! Come, Miss Proserpine : cant you find a date for the costers ? What about the 25th ? that was vacant the day before yesterday.

PROSERPINE [*referring to diary*] Engaged — the Fabian Society.

MORELL. Bother the Fabian Society ! Is the 28th gone too ?

PROSERPINE. City dinner. Youre invited to dine with the Founders' Company.

MORELL. Thatll do : I'll go to the Hoxton Group of Freedom instead. [*She enters the engagement in silence, with implacable disparagement of the Hoxton Anarchists in every line of her face. Morell bursts open the cover of a copy of The Church Reformer, which has come by post, and glances through Mr Stewart Headlam's leader and the Guild of St Matthew news. These proceedings are presently enlivened by the appearance of Morell's curate, the Reverend Alexander Mill, a young gentleman gathered by Morell from the nearest University settlement, whither he had come from Oxford to give the east end of London the benefit of his university training. He is a conceitedly well intentioned, enthusiastic, immature person, with nothing positively unbearable about him except a habit of speaking with his lips carefully closed a full half inch from each corner for the sake of a finicking articulation and a set of horribly corrupt vowels, notably ow for o, this being his chief means of bringing Oxford refinement to bear on Hackney vulgarity. Morell, whom he has won over by a doglike devotion, looks up indulgently from The Church Reformer, and remarks]* Well, Lexy? Late again, as usual!

LEXY. I'm afraid so. I wish I could get up in the morning.

MORELL [*exulting in his own energy*] Ha! ha! [*Whimsically*] Watch and pray, Lexy: watch and pray.

LEXY. I know. [*Rising wittily to the occasion*] But how can I watch and pray when I am asleep? Isnt that so, Miss Prossy?

PROSERPINE [*sharply*] Miss Garnett, if you please.

LEXY. I beg your pardon — Miss Garnett.

PROSERPINE. Youve got to do all the work to-day.

LEXY. Why?

PROSERPINE. Never mind why. It will do you good to earn your supper before you eat it, for once in a way, as I do. Come: dont dawdle. You should have been off on your rounds half an hour ago.

LEXY [*perplexed*] Is she in earnest, Morell?

MORELL [*in the highest spirits — his eyes dancing*] Yes. I am going to dawdle to-day.

LEXY. You! You dont know how.

MORELL [*heartily*] Ha! ha! Dont I? I'm going to have this day all to myself — or at least the forenoon. My wife's coming back: she's due here at 11.45.

LEXY [*surprised*] Coming back already — with the children? I thought they were to stay to the end of the month.

MORELL. So they are: she's only coming up for two days, to get some flannel things for Jimmy, and to see how we're getting on without her.

LEXY [*anxiously*] But, my dear Morell, if what Jimmy and Fluffy had was scarlatina, do you think it wise—

MORELL. Scarlatina! — rubbish, German measles. I brought it into the house myself from the Pycroft Street

School. A parson is like a doctor, my boy : he must face infection as a soldier must face bullets. [*He rises and claps Lexy on the shoulder*] Catch the measles if you can, Lexy : she'll nurse you ; and what a piece of luck that will be for you ! Eh ?

LEXY [*smiling uneasily*] It's so hard to understand you about Mrs Morell—

MORELL [*tenderly*] Ah, my boy, get married — get married to a good woman ; and then youll understand. Thats a foretaste of what will be best in the Kingdom of Heaven we are trying to establish on earth. That will cure you of dawdling. An honest man feels that he must pay Heaven for every hour of happiness with a good spell of hard, unselfish work to make others happy. We have no more right to consume happiness without producing it than to consume wealth without producing it. Get a wife like my Candida ; and youll always be in arrear with your repayment. [*He pats Lexy affectionately on the back, and is leaving the room when Lexy calls to him*].

LEXY. Oh, wait a bit : I forgot. [*Morell halts and turns with the door knob in his hand*]. Your father-in-law is coming round to see you. [*Morell shuts the door again, with a complete change of manner*].

MORELL [*surprised and not pleased*] Mr Burgess ?

LEXY. Yes. I passed him in the park, arguing with somebody. He gave me good day and asked me to let you know that he was coming.

MORELL [*half incredulous*] But he hasnt called here for — I may almost say for years. Are you sure, Lexy ? Youre not joking, are you ?

LEXY [*earnestly*] No sir, really.

MORELL [*thoughtfully*] Hm ! Time for him to take another look at Candida before she grows out of his knowledge. [*He resigns himself to the inevitable, and goes out. Lexy looks after him with beaming, foolish worship. Miss Garnett, not being able to shake Lexy, relieves her feelings by worrying the typewriter*].

LEXY. What a good man ! What a thorough, loving soul he is ! [*He takes Morell's place at the table, making himself very comfortable as he takes out a cigaret*].

PROSERPINE [*impatiently, pulling the letter she has been working at off the typewriter and folding it*] Oh, a man ought to be able to be fond of his wife without making a fool of himself about her.

LEXY [*shocked*] Oh, Miss Prossy !

PROSERPINE [*rising busily and coming to the stationery case to get an envelope, in which she encloses the letter as she speaks*] Candida here, and Candida there, and Candida everywhere ! [*She licks the envelope*]. It's enough to drive anyone out of their s e n s e s [*thumping the envelope to make it stick*] to hear a perfectly commonplace woman raved about in that absurd manner merely because she's got good hair, and a tolerable figure.

LEXY [*with reproachful gravity*] I think her extremely beautiful, Miss Garnett. [*He takes the photograph up ; looks at it ; and adds, with even greater impressiveness*] e x - t r e m e l y beautiful. How fine her eyes are !

PROSERPINE. Her eyes are not a bit better than mine — now ! [*He puts down the photograph and stares austerely at her*]. And you know very well that you think me dowdy and second rate enough.

LEXY [*rising majestically*] Heaven forbid that I should think of any of God's creatures in such a way ! [*He moves stiffly away from her across the room to the neighborhood of the bookcase*].

PROSERPINE [*sarcastically*] Thank you. Thats very nice and comforting.

LEXY [*saddened by her depravity*] I had no idea you had any feeling against Mrs Morell.

PROSERPINE [*indignantly*] I have no feeling against her. She's very nice, very good-hearted : I'm very fond of her, and can appreciate her real qualities far better than any man can. [*He shakes his head sadly and turns to the bookcase, looking along the shelves for a volume. She follows him with intense pepperiness*] You dont believe me? [*He turns and faces her. She pounces at him with spitfire energy*] You think I'm jealous? Oh, what a profound knowledge of the human heart you have, Mr Lexy Mill! How well you know the weaknesses of Woman, dont you? It must be so nice to be a man and have a fine penetrating intellect instead of mere emotions like us, and to know that the reason we dont share your amorous delusions is that we're all jealous of one another! [*She abandons him with a toss of her shoulders, and crosses to the fire to warm her hands*].

LEXY. Ah, if you women only had the same clue to Man's strength that you have to his weakness, Miss Prossy, there would be no Woman Question.

PROSERPINE [*over her shoulder, as she stoops, holding her hands to the blaze*] Where did you hear Morell say that? You didnt invent it yourself: youre not clever enough.

LEXY. Thats quite true. I am not ashamed of owing him that, as I owe him so many other spiritual truths. He said it at the annual conference of the Women's Liberal Federation. Allow me to add that though they didnt appreciate it, I, a mere man, did. [*He turns to the bookcase again, hoping that this may leave her crushed*].

PROSERPINE [*putting her hair straight at the little panel of mirror in the mantelpiece*] Well, when you talk to me, give me your own ideas, such as they are, and not his. You never cut a poorer figure than when you are trying to imitate him.

LEXY [*stung*] I try to follow his example, not to imitate him.

PROSERPINE [*coming at him again on her way back to her work*] Yes, you do: you imitate him. Why do you tuck your umbrella under your left arm instead of carrying it in your hand like anyone else? Why do you walk with your chin stuck out before you, hurrying along with that eager look in your eyes? you! who never get up before half past nine in the morning. Why do you say "knoa-

ledge" in church, though you always say "knolledge" in
private conversation ! Bah ! do you think I dont know ?
[*She goes back to the typewriter*]. Here : come and set about
your work : weve wasted enough time for one morning.
Here's a copy of the diary for to-day. [*She hands him a
memorandum*].

LEXY [*deeply offended*] Thank you. [*He takes it and
stands at the table with his back to her, reading it. She begins
to transcribe her shorthand notes on the typewriter without
troubling herself about his feelings. Mr Burgess enters un-
announced. He is a man of sixty, made coarse and sordid by
the compulsory selfishness of petty commerce, and later on soft-
ened into sluggish bumptiousness by overfeeding and commercial
success. A vulgar, ignorant, guzzling man, offensive and
contemptuous to people whose labor is cheap, respectful to wealth
and rank, and quite sincere and without rancor or envy in both
attitudes. Finding him without talent, the world has offered
him no decently paid work except ignoble work ; and he has
become, in consequence, somewhat hoggish. But he has no
suspicion of this himself, and honestly regards his commercial
prosperity as the inevitable and socially wholesome triumph of
the ability, industry, shrewdness and experience in business of a
man who in private is easygoing, affectionate and humorously
convivial to a fault. Corporeally, he is podgy, with a snoutish
nose in the centre of a flat, square face ; a dust colored beard,
with a patch of grey in the centre, under his chin ; and small
watery blue eyes with a plaintively sentimental expression,
which he transfers easily to his voice by his habit of pompously
intoning his sentences*].

BURGESS [*stopping on the threshold, and looking round*] They
told me Mr Morell was here.

PROSERPINE [*rising*] He's upstairs. I'll fetch him for
you.

BURGESS [*staring boorishly at her*] Youre not the same
young lady as hused to typewrite for him ?

PROSERPINE. No.

BURGESS [*assenting*] No : she was young-er. [*Miss Gar-*

*nett stares at him; then goes out with great dignity. He
receives this obtusely, and crosses to the hearth-rug, where he
turns and spreads himself with his back to the fire*]. Startin
on your rounds, Mr Mill?

LEXY [*folding his paper and pocketing it*] Yes : I must be
off presently.

BURGESS [*momentously*] Dont let me detain you, Mr Mill.
What I come about is private between me and Mr
Morell.

LEXY [*huffily*] I have no intention of intruding, I am
sure, Mr Burgess. Good morning.

BURGESS [*patronizingly*] Oh, good morning to you.

Morell returns as Lexy is making for the door.

MORELL [*to Lexy*] Off to work?

LEXY. Yes, sir.

MORELL [*patting him affectionately on the shoulder*] Take
my silk handkerchief and wrap your throat up.   Theres a
cold wind.   Away with you.   [*Lexy, more than consoled for
Burgess's rudeness, brightens up, and goes out*].

BURGESS. Spoilin your korates [curates], as usu'l, James.
Good mornin.   When I pay a man, an' 'is livin depens on
me, I keep him in 'is place.

MORELL [*rather shortly*] I always keep my curates in their
places as my helpers and comrades.   If you get as much
work out of your clerks and warehousemen as I do out of
my curates, you must be getting rich pretty fast.   Will
you take your old chair.

*He points with curt authority to the armchair beside the
fireplace; then takes the spare chair from the table and sits
down at an unfamiliar distance from his visitor.*

BURGESS [*without moving*] Just the same as hever, James!

MORELL. When you last called — it was about three
years ago, I think — you said the same thing a little more
frankly.   Your exact words then were : "Just as big a
fool as ever, James!"

BURGESS [*soothingly*] Well, praps I did; but [*with
conciliatory cheerfulness*] I meant no hoffence by it.   A

clorgyman is privileged to be a bit of a fool, you know : it's ony becomin in 'is profession that he should.   Anyhow, I come here, not to rake up hold differences, but to let bygones be bygones.   [*Suddenly becoming very solemn, and approaching Morell*] James : three year ago, you done me a hill turn.   You done me hout of a contrac ; an when I gev you arsh words in my natral disappointment, you turned my daughrter again me.   Well, Ive come to hact the part of a Kerischin.   [*Offering his hand*] I forgive you, James.

MORELL [*starting up*] Confound your impudence !

BURGESS [*retreating, with almost lachrymose deprecation of this treatment*] Is that becomin language for a clorgyman, James ? — and you so particlar, too ?

MORELL [*hotly*] No, sir, it is not becoming language for a clergyman.   I used the wrong word.   I should have said damn your impudence : thats what St Paul or any honest priest would have said to you.   Do you think I have forgotten that tender of yours for the contract to supply clothing to the workhouse ?

BURGESS [*in a paroxysm of public spirit*] I hacted in the hinterest of the ratepayers, James.   It was the lowest tender : you carnt deny that.

MORELL.   Yes, the lowest, because you paid worse wages than any other employer — starvation wages — aye, worse than starvation wages — to the women who made the clothing.   Your wages would have driven them to the streets to keep body and soul together.   [*Getting angrier and angrier*] Those women were my parishioners.   I shamed the Guardians out of accepting your tender : I shamed the ratepayers out of letting them do it : I shamed everybody but you.   [*Boiling over*] How dare you, sir, come here and offer to forgive me, and talk about your daughter, and—

BURGESS.   Heasy, James, heasy, heasy !   Dont git hinto a fluster about nothink.   Ive howned I was wrong.

MORELL [*fuming about*] Have you ?   I didnt hear you.

BURGESS. Of course I did. I hown it now. Come : I harsk your pardon for the letter I wrote you. Is that enough ?

MORELL [*snapping his fingers*] Thats nothing. Have you raised the wages ?

BURGESS [*triumphantly*] Yes.

MORELL [*stopping dead*] What !

BURGESS [*unctuously*] Ive turned a moddle hemployer. I dont hemploy no women now : theyre all sacked ; and the work is done by machinery. Not a man 'as less than six-pence a *h*our ; and the skilled ands gits the Trade Union rate. [*Proudly*] What ave you to say to me now ?

MORELL [*overwhelmed*] Is it possible ! Well, theres more joy in heaven over one sinner that repenteth— [*Going to Burgess with an explosion of apologetic cordiality*] My dear Burgess: I most heartily beg your pardon for my hard thoughts of you. [*Grasping his hand*] And now, dont you feel the better for the change ? Come, confess : youre happier. You look happier.

BURGESS [*ruefully*] Well, praps I do. I spose I must, since you notice it. At all events, I git my contrax asseppit [accepted] by the County Council. [*Savagely*] They dussent ave nothink to do with me unless I paid fair wages — curse em for a parcel o meddlin fools !

MORELL [*dropping his hand, utterly discouraged*] So that was why you raised the wages ! [*He sits down moodily*].

BURGESS [*severely, in spreading, mounting tones*] Why helse should I do it ? What does it lead to but drink and hup-pishness in workin men ? [*He seats himself magisterially in the easy chair*]. It's hall very well for you, James : it gits you hinto the papers and makes a great man of you ; but you never think of the arm you do, puttin money into the pockets of workin men that they dunno ow to spend, and takin it from people that might be makin a good huse on it.

MORELL [*with a heavy sigh, speaking with cold politeness*] What is your business with me this morning ? I shall not pretend to believe that you are here merely out of family sentiment.

BURGESS [*obstinately*] Yes, I ham : just family sentiment and nothink helse.

MORELL [*with weary calm*] I dont believe you.

BURGESS [*rising threateningly*] Dont say that to me again, James Mavor Morell.

MORELL [*unmoved*] I'll say it just as often as may be necessary to convince you that it's true. I dont believe you.

BURGESS [*collapsing into an abyss of wounded feeling*] Oh, well, if youre detormined to be hunfriendly, I spose I'd better go. [*He moves reluctantly towards the door. Morell makes no sign. He lingers*]. I didnt hexpect to find a hunforgivin spirit in you, James. [*Morell still not responding, he takes a few more reluctant steps doorwards. Then he comes back, whining*]. We huseter git on well enough, spite of our different hopinions. Why are you so changed to me ? I give you my word I come here in peeorr [pure] frenliness, not wishin to be on bad terms with my hown daughrter's usban. Come, James : be a Kerischin, and shake ands. [*He puts his hand sentimentally on Morell's shoulder*].

MORELL [*looking up at him thoughtfully*] Look here, Burgess. Do you want to be as welcome here as you were before you lost that contract ?

BURGESS. I do, James. I do — *h*onest.

MORELL. Then why dont you behave as you did then ?

BURGESS [*cautiously removing his hand*] Ow d'y'mean ?

MORELL. I'll tell you. You thought me a young fool then.

BURGESS [*coaxingly*] No I didnt, James. I—

MORELL [*cutting him short*] Yes, you did. And I thought you an old scoundrel.

BURGESS [*most vehemently deprecating this gross self-accusation on Morell's part*] No you didnt, James. Now you do yourself a hinjustice.

MORELL. Yes I did. Well, that did not prevent our

getting on very well together. God made you what I call
a scoundrel as He made me what you call a fool. [*The
effect of this observation on Burgess is to remove the keystone
of his moral arch. He becomes bodily weak, and, with his eyes
fixed on Morell in a helpless stare, puts out his hand apprehensively to balance himself, as if the floor had suddenly sloped
under him. Morell proceeds, in the same tone of quiet conviction*] It was not for me to quarrel with His handiwork in
the one case more than in the other. So long as you come
here honestly as a self-respecting, thorough, convinced
scoundrel, justifying your scoundrelism, and proud of it,
you are welcome. But [*and now Morell's tone becomes for-
midable; and he rises and strikes the back of the chair for
greater emphasis*] I wont have you here snivelling about
being a model employer and a converted man when youre
only an apostate with your coat turned for the sake of a
County Council contract. [*He nods at him to enforce the
point; then goes to the hearth-rug, where he takes up a comfortably commanding position with his back to the fire, and con-
tinues*] No : I like a man to be true to himself, even in
wickedness. Come now : either take your hat and go ;
or else sit down and give me a good scoundrelly reason for
wanting to be friends with me. [*Burgess, whose emotions
have subsided sufficiently to be expressed by a dazed grin, is
relieved by this concrete proposition. He ponders it for a
moment, and then, slowly and very modestly, sits down in the
chair Morell has just left*]. Thats right. Now, out with it.

BURGESS [*chuckling in spite of himself*] Well, you orr a
queer bird, James, and no mistake. But [*almost enthusias-
tically*] one carnt elp likin you : besides, as I said afore, of
course one dont take hall a clorgyman says seriously, or the
world couldnt go on. Could it now ? [*He composes himself
for graver discourse, and, turning his eyes on Morell, proceeds
with dull seriousness*] Well, I dont mind tellin you, since
it's your wish we should be free with hwun another, that I
did think you a bit of a fool once ; but I'm beginnin to
think that praps I was be'ind the times a bit.

MORELL [*exultant*] Aha !   Youre finding that out at last, are you ?

BURGESS [*portentously*] Yes : times 'as changed mor'n I could a believed.   Five yorr [year] ago, no sensible man would a thought o takin hup with your hidears.   I hused to wonder you was let preach at all.   Why, I know a clorgyman what 'as bin kep hout of his job for yorrs by the Bishop o London, although the pore feller's not a bit more religious than you are.   But to-day, if hennyone was to orffer to bet me a thousan poun that youll hend by bein a bishop yourself, I dussent take the bet.   [*Very impressively*] You and yore crew are gettin hinfluential : I can see that. Theyll ave to give you somethink someday, if it's honly to stop yore mouth.   You ad the right instinc arter all, James : the line you took is the payin line in the long run fur a man o your sort.

MORELL [*offering his hand with thorough decision*] Shake hands, Burgess.   Now youre talking honestly.   I dont think theyll make me a bishop ; but if they do, I'll introduce you to the biggest jobbers I can get to come to my dinner parties.

BURGESS [*who has risen with a sheepish grin and accepted the hand of friendship*] You will ave your joke, James.   Our quarrel's made up now, ain it ?

A WOMAN'S VOICE. Say yes, James.

Startled, they turn quickly and find that Candida has just come in, and is looking at them with an amused maternal indulgence which is her characteristic expression. She is a woman of 33, well built, well nourished, likely, one guesses, to become matronly later on, but now quite at her best, with the double charm of youth and motherhood. Her ways are those of a woman who has found that she can always manage people by engaging their affection, and who does so frankly and instinctively without the smallest scruple. So far, she is like any other pretty woman who is just clever enough to make the most of her sexual attractions for trivially selfish ends ; but Candida's serene brow, courageous eyes, and well set mouth and chin

He is afraid of Burgess, and would run away into solitude if he dared; but the very intensity with which he feels a perfectly commonplace position comes from excessive nervous force; and his nostrils, mouth, and eyes betray a fiercely petulant wilfulness, as to the bent of which his brow, already lined with pity, is reassuring. He is so uncommon as to be almost unearthly; and to prosaic people there is something noxious in this unearthliness, just as to poetic people there is something angelic in it. His dress is anarchic. He wears an old blue serge jacket, unbuttoned, over a woollen lawn tennis shirt, with a silk handkerchief for a cravat, trousers matching the jacket, and brown canvas shoes. In these garments he has apparently lain in the heather and waded through the waters; and there is no evidence of his having ever brushed them.

As he catches sight of a stranger on entering, he stops, and edges along the wall on the opposite side of the room.

MORELL [*as he enters*] Come along : you can spare us quarter of an hour, at all events. This is my father-in-law, Mr Burgess — Mr Marchbanks.

MARCHBANKS [*nervously backing against the bookcase*] Glad to meet you, sir.

BURGESS [*crossing to him with great heartiness, whilst Morell joins Candida at the fire*] Glad to meet you, I'm shore, Mr Morchbanks. [*Forcing him to shake hands*] Ow do you find yoreself this weather? Ope you aint lettin James put no foolish ideas into your ed?

MARCHBANKS. Foolish ideas? Oh, you mean Socialism! No.

BURGESS. Thats right. [*Again looking at his watch*] Well, I must go now : theres no elp for it. Yore not comin my way, are you, Mr Morchbanks?

MARCHBANKS. Which way is that?

BURGESS. Victawriar Pawrk Station. Theres a city train at 12.25.

MORELL. Nonsense. Eugene will stay to lunch with us, I expect.

MARCHBANKS [*anxiously excusing himself*] No — I — I—

BURGESS. Well, well, I shornt press you : I bet youd

rather lunch with Candy. Some night, I ope, youll come and dine with me at my club, the Freeman Founders in Nortn Folgit. Come : say you will !

MARCHBANKS. Thank you, Mr Burgess. Where is Norton Folgate — down in Surrey, isnt it ? [*Burgess, inexpressibly tickled, begins to splutter with laughter*].

CANDIDA [*coming to the rescue*] Youll lose your train, papa, if you dont go at once. Come back in the afternoon and tell Mr Marchbanks where to find the club.

BURGESS [*roaring with glee*] Down in Surrey — har, har ! thats not a bad one. Well, I never met a man as didnt know Nortn Folgit afore. [*Abashed at his own noisiness*] Good-bye, Mr Morchbanks : I know yore too ighbred to take my pleasantry in bad part. [*He again offers his hand*].

MARCHBANKS [*taking it with a nervous jerk*] Not at all.

BURGESS. Bye, bye, Candy. I'll look in again later on. So long, James.

MORELL. Must you go ?

BURGESS. Dont stir. [*He goes out with unabated heartiness*].

MORELL. Oh, I'll see you off. [*He follows him. Eugene stares after them apprehensively, holding his breath until Burgess disappears*].

CANDIDA [*laughing*] Well, Eugene ? [*He turns with a start, and comes eagerly towards her, but stops irresolutely as he meets her amused look*]. What do you think of my father ?

MARCHBANKS. I — I hardly know him yet. He seems to be a very nice old gentleman.

CANDIDA [*with gentle irony*] And youll go to the Freeman Founders to dine with him, wont you ?

MARCHBANKS [*miserably, taking it quite seriously*] Yes, if it will please you.

CANDIDA [*touched*] Do you know, you are a very nice boy, Eugene, with all your queerness. If you had laughed at my father I shouldnt have minded ; but I like you ever so much better for being nice to him.

MARCHBANKS. Ought I to have laughed ?   I noticed that he said something funny ; but I am so ill at ease with strangers ; and I never can see a joke.   I'm very sorry. [*He sits down on the sofa, his elbows on his knees and his temples between his fists, with an expression of hopeless suffering*].

CANDIDA [*bustling him goodnaturedly*] Oh, come !   You great baby, you !   You are worse than usual this morning. Why were you so melancholy as we came along in the cab ?

MARCHBANKS. Oh, that was nothing.   I was wondering how much I ought to give the cabman.   I know it's utterly silly ; but you dont know how dreadful such things are to me — how I shrink from having to deal with strange people.   [*Quickly and reassuringly*] But it's all right.   He beamed all over and touched his hat when Morell gave him two shillings.   I was on the point of offering him ten.   [*Candida laughs heartily.   Morell comes back with a few letters and newspapers which have come by the midday post*].

CANDIDA. Oh, James dear, he was going to give the cabman ten shillings — ten shillings for a three minutes drive ! Oh dear !

MORELL [*at the table, glancing through the letters*] Never mind her, Marchbanks.   The overpaying instinct is a generous one : better than the underpaying instinct, and not so common.

MARCHBANKS [*relapsing into dejection*] No : cowardice, incompetence.   Mrs Morell's quite right.

CANDIDA. Of course she is.   [*She takes up her hand-bag*]. And now I must leave you to James for the present.   I suppose you are too much of a poet to know the state a woman finds her house in when she's been away for three weeks.   Give me my rug.   [*Eugene takes the strapped rug from the couch, and gives it to her.   She takes it in her left hand, having the bag in her right*]. Now hang my cloak across my arm. [*He obeys*]. Now my hat. [*He puts it into the hand which has the bag*]. Now open the door for me. [*He hurries before her and opens the door*]. Thanks. [*She goes out; and Marchbanks shuts the door*].

MORELL [*still busy at the table*] Youll stay to lunch, Marchbanks, of course.

MARCHBANKS [*scared*] I musnt. [*He glances quickly at Morell, but at once avoids his frank look, and adds, with obvious disingenuousness*] I mean I cant.

MORELL. You mean you wont.

MARCHBANKS [*earnestly*] No : I should like to, indeed. Thank you very much. But — but—

MORELL [*breezily, finishing with the letters and coming close to him*] But — but — but — but — Bosh ! If youd like to stay, stay. You dont mean to persuade me you have anything else to do. If youre shy, go and take a turn in the park and write poetry until half past one ; and then come in and have a good feed.

MARCHBANKS. Thank you, I should like that very much. But I really musnt. The truth is, Mrs Morell told me not to. She said she didnt think youd ask me to stay to lunch, but that I was to remember, if you did, that you didnt really want me to. [*Plaintively*] She said I'd understand ; but I dont. Please dont tell her I told you.

MORELL [*drolly*] Oh, is that all ? Wont my suggestion that you should take a turn in the park meet the difficulty ?

MARCHBANKS. How ?

MORELL [*exploding good-humoredly*] Why, you duffer— [*But this boisterousness jars himself as well as Eugene. He checks himself, and resumes, with affectionate seriousness*] No : I wont put it in that way. My dear lad : in a happy marriage like ours, there is something very sacred in the return of the wife to her home. [*Marchbanks looks quickly at him, half anticipating his meaning*]. An old friend or a truly noble and sympathetic soul is not in the way on such occasions ; but a chance visitor is. [*The hunted, horror-stricken expression comes out with sudden vividness in Eugene's face as he understands. Morell, occupied with his own thought, goes on without noticing this*]. Candida thought I would rather not have you here ; but she was wrong. I'm very fond of you, my boy ; and I should like you to see for yourself what a happy thing it is to be married as I am.

MARCHBANKS. Happy ! — your marriage ! You think that ! You believe that !

MORELL [*buoyantly*] I know it, my lad. Larochefoucauld said that there are convenient marriages, but no delightful ones. You dont know the comfort of seeing through and through a thundering liar and rotten cynic like that fellow. Ha, ha ! Now, off with you to the park, and write your poem. Half past one, sharp, mind : we never wait for anybody.

MARCHBANKS [*wildly*] No : stop : you shant. I'll force it into the light.

MORELL [*puzzled*] Eh ? Force what ?

MARCHBANKS. I must speak to you. There is something that must be settled between us.

MORELL [*with a whimsical glance at the clock*] Now ?

MARCHBANKS [*passionately*] Now. Before you leave this room. [*He retreats a few steps, and stands as if to bar Morell's way to the door*].

MORELL [*without moving, and gravely, perceiving now that there is something serious the matter*] I'm not going to leave it, my dear boy : I thought you were. [*Eugene, baffled by his firm tone, turns his back on him, writhing with anger. Morell goes to him and puts his hand on his shoulder strongly and kindly, disregarding his attempt to shake it off*]. Come : sit down quietly ; and tell me what it is. And remember : we are friends, and need not fear that either of us will be anything but patient and kind to the other, whatever we may have to say.

of delivery] You will be married ; and you will be working with all your might and valor to make every spot on
earth as happy as your own home. You will be one of
the makers of the Kingdom of Heaven on earth ; and —
who knows ? — you may be a pioneer and master builder
where I am only a humble journeyman ; for dont think,
my boy, that I cannot see in you, young as you are,
promise of higher powers than I can ever pretend to. I
well know that it is in the poet that the holy spirit of man
— the god within him — is most godlike. It should make
you tremble to think of that — to think that the heavy
burthen and great gift of a poet may be laid upon
you.

MARCHBANKS [*unimpressed and remorseless, his boyish
crudity of assertion telling sharply against Morell's oratory*] It
does not make me tremble. It is the want of it in others
that makes me tremble.

MORELL [*redoubling his force of style under the stimulus of
his genuine feeling and Eugene's obduracy*] Then help to
kindle it in them — in me — not to extinguish it. In
the future — when you are as happy as I am — I will be
your true brother in the faith. I will help you to believe
that God has given us a world that nothing but our own
folly keeps from being a paradise. I will help you to
believe that every stroke of your work is sowing happiness
for the great harvest that all — even the humblest — shall
one day reap. And last, but trust me, not least, I will
help you to believe that your wife loves you and is happy
in her home. We need such help, Marchbanks : we need
it greatly and always. There are so many things to make us
doubt, if once we let our understanding be troubled. Even
at home, we sit as if in camp, encompassed by a hostile
army of doubts. Will you play the traitor and let them
in on me ?

MARCHBANKS [*looking round him*] Is it like this for
her here always ? A woman, with a great soul, craving
for reality, truth, freedom ; and being fed on metaphors,

sermons, stale perorations, mere rhetoric. Do you think a woman's soul can live on your talent for preaching?

MORELL [*stung*] Marchbanks : you make it hard for me to control myself. My talent is like yours insofar as it has any real worth at all. It is the gift of finding words for divine truth.

MARCHBANKS [*impetuously*] It's the gift of the gab, nothing more and nothing less. What has your knack of fine talking to do with the truth, anymore than playing the organ has? Ive never been in your church ; but Ive been to your political meetings ; and Ive seen you do whats called rousing the meeting to enthusiasm : that is, you excited them until they behaved exactly as if they were drunk. And their wives looked on and saw what fools they were. Oh, it's an old story : youll find it in the Bible. I imagine King David, in his fits of enthusiasm, was very like you. [*Stabbing him with the words*] " But his wife despised him in her heart."

MORELL [*wrathfully*] Leave my house. Do you hear? [*He advances on him threateningly*].

MARCHBANKS [*shrinking back against the couch*] Let me alone. Dont touch me. [*Morell grasps him powerfully by the lappell of his coat : he cowers down on the sofa and screams passionately*] Stop, Morell : if you strike me, I'll kill myself : I wont bear it. [*Almost in hysterics*] Let me go. Take your hand away.

MORELL [*with slow, emphatic scorn*] You little snivelling, cowardly whelp. [*He releases him*]. Go, before you frighten yourself into a fit.

MARCHBANKS [*on the sofa, gasping, but relieved by the withdrawal of Morell's hand*] I'm not afraid of you : it's you who are afraid of me.

MORELL [*quietly, as he stands over him*] It looks like it, doesnt it?

MARCHBANKS [*with petulant vehemence*] Yes, it does. [*Morell turns away contemptuously. Eugene scrambles to his feet and follows him*]. You think because I shrink from being brutally handled — because [*with tears in his voice*] I can do nothing but cry with rage when I am met with violence — because I cant lift a heavy trunk down from the top of a cab like you — because I cant fight you for your wife as a navvy would : all that makes you think that I'm afraid of you. But youre wrong. If I havnt got what you call British pluck, I havnt British cowardice either : I'm not afraid of a clergyman's ideas. I'll fight your ideas. I'll rescue her from her slavery to them : I'll pit my own ideas against them. You are driving me out of the house because you darent let her choose between your ideas and mine. You are afraid to let me see her again. [*Morell, angered, turns suddenly on him. He flies to the door in involuntary dread*]. Let me alone, I say. I'm going.

MORELL [*with cold scorn*] Wait a moment: I am not going to touch you: dont be afraid. When my wife comes back she will want to know why you have gone. And when she finds that you are never going to cross our threshold again, she will want to have that explained too. Now I dont wish to distress her by telling her that you have behaved like a blackguard.

MARCHBANKS [*coming back with renewed vehemence*] You shall — you must. If you give any explanation but the true one, you are a liar and a coward. Tell her what I said ; and how you were strong and manly, and shook me as a terrier shakes a rat ; and how I shrank and was terrified ; and how you called me a snivelling little whelp and put me out of the house. If you dont tell her, I will : I'll write it to her.

MORELL [*taken aback*] Why do you want her to know this ?

MARCHBANKS [*with lyric rapture*] Because she will understand me, and know that I understand her. If you keep back one word of it from her — if you are not ready to lay the truth at her feet as I am — then you will know to the end of your days that she really belongs to me and not to you. Good-bye. [*Going*].

MORELL [*terribly disquieted*] Stop : I will not tell her.

MARCHBANKS [*turning near the door*] Either the truth or a lie you must tell her, if I go.

MORELL [*temporizing*] Marchbanks : it is sometimes justifiable—

MARCHBANKS [*cutting him short*] I know — to lie. It will be useless. Good-bye, Mr Clergyman.

As he turns finally to the door, it opens and Candida enters in her housekeeping dress.

CANDIDA. Are you going, Eugene ? [*Looking more observantly at him*] Well, dear me, just look at you, going out into the street in that state ! You are a poet, certainly. Look at him, James ! [*She takes him by the coat, and brings him forward, shewing him to Morell*]. Look at his collar ! look at his tie ! look at his hair ! One would think somebody had been throttling you. [*The two men guard themselves against betraying their consciousness*]. Here ! Stand still. [*She buttons his collar ; ties his neckerchief in a bow ; and arranges his hair*]. There ! Now you look so nice that I think youd better stay to lunch after all, though I told you you musnt. It will be ready in half an hour. [*She puts a final touch to the bow. He kisses her hand*]. Dont be silly.

MARCHBANKS. I want to stay, of course — unless the reverend gentleman your husband has anything to advance to the contrary.

CANDIDA. Shall he stay, James, if he promises to be a good boy and to help me to lay the table ? [*Marchbanks turns his head and looks steadfastly at Morell over his shoulder, challenging his answer*].

MORELL [*shortly*] Oh yes, certainly : he had better. [*He goes to the table and pretends to busy himself with his papers there*].

MARCHBANKS [*offering his arm to Candida*] Come and lay the table. [*She takes it. They go to the door together. As they pass out he adds*] I am the happiest of mortals.

MORELL. So was I — an hour ago.

ACT II

*The same day. The same room. Late in the afternoon.
The chair for Morell's visitors has been replaced at the table,
which is, if possible, more untidy than before. Marchbanks,
alone and idle, is trying to find out how the typewriter works.
Hearing someone at the door, he steals guiltily away to the
window and pretends to be absorbed in the view. Miss Garnett,
carrying the notebook in which she takes down Morell's letters
in shorthand from his dictation, sits down at the typewriter and
sets to work transcribing them, much too busy to notice Eugene.
Unfortunately the first key she strikes sticks.*

PROSERPINE. Bother! Youve been meddling with my
typewriter, Mr Marchbanks; and theres not the least
use in your trying to look as if you hadnt.

MARCHBANKS [*timidly*] I'm very sorry, Miss Garnett. I
only tried to make it write.

PROSERPINE. Well, youve made this key stick.

MARCHBANKS [*earnestly*] I assure you I didnt touch the
keys. I didnt indeed. I only turned a little wheel. [*He
points irresolutely at the tension wheel*].

PROSERPINE. Oh, now I understand. [*She sets the
machine to rights, talking volubly all the time*]. I suppose
you thought it was a sort of barrel-organ. Nothing to do
but turn the handle, and it would write a beautiful love
letter for you straight off, eh?

MARCHBANKS [*seriously*] I suppose a machine could be

made to write love-letters.   Theyre all the same, arnt they?

PROSERPINE [*somewhat indignantly: any such discussion, except by way of pleasantry, being outside her code of manners*] How do I know?   Why do you ask me?

MARCHBANKS. I beg your pardon.   I thought clever people — people who can do business and write letters, and that sort of thing — always had love affairs.

PROSERPINE [*rising, outraged*] Mr Marchbanks!   [*She looks severely at him, and marches with much dignity to the bookcase*].

MARCHBANKS [*approaching her humbly*] I hope I havnt offended you.   Perhaps I shouldnt have alluded to your love affairs.

PROSERPINE [*plucking a blue book from the shelf and turning sharply on him*] I havnt any love affairs.   How dare you say such a thing?

MARCHBANKS [*simply*] Really!   Oh, then you are shy, like me.   Isnt that so?

PROSERPINE. Certainly I am not shy.   What do you mean?

MARCHBANKS [*secretly*] You must be : that is the reason there are so few love affairs in the world.   We all go about longing for love : it is the first need of our natures, the first prayer of our hearts ; but we dare not utter our longing : we are too shy.   [*Very earnestly*] Oh, Miss Garnett, what would you not give to be without fear, without shame—

PROSERPINE [*scandalized*] Well, upon my word!

MARCHBANKS [*with petulant impatience*] Ah, dont say those stupid things to me : they dont deceive me : what use are they?   Why are you afraid to be your real self with me?   I am just like you.

PROSERPINE. Like me!   Pray are you flattering me or flattering yourself?   I dont feel quite sure which.   [*She turns to go back to the typewriter*].

MARCHBANKS [*stopping her mysteriously*] Hush!   I go

about in search of love ; and I find it in unmeasured stores in the bosoms of others. But when I try to ask for it, this horrible shyness strangles me ; and I stand dumb, or, worse than dumb, saying meaningless things — foolish lies. And I see the affection I am longing for given to dogs and cats and pet birds, because they come and ask for it. [*Almost whispering*] It must be asked for : it is like a ghost : it cannot speak unless it is first spoken to. [*At his usual pitch, but with deep melancholy*] All the love in the world is longing to speak ; only it dare not, because it is shy ! shy ! shy ! That is the world's tragedy. [*With a deep sigh he sits in the visitors' chair and buries his face in his hands*].

PROSERPINE [*amazed, but keeping her wits about her — her point of honor in encounters with strange young men*] Wicked people get over that shyness occasionally, dont they ?

MARCHBANKS [*scrambling up almost fiercely*] Wicked people means people who have no love : therefore they have no shame. They have the power to ask love because they dont need it : they have the power to offer it because they have none to give. [*He collapses into his seat, and adds, mournfully*] But we, who have love, and long to mingle it with the love of others : we cannot utter a word. [*Timidly*] You find that, dont you ?

PROSERPINE. Look here : if you dont stop talking like this, I'll leave the room, Mr Marchbanks : I really will. It's not proper.

She resumes her seat at the typewriter, opening the blue book and preparing to copy a passage from it.

MARCHBANKS [*hopelessly*] Nothing thats worth saying is proper. [*He rises, and wanders about the room in his lost way, saying*] I cant understand you, Miss Garnett. What am I to talk about ?

PROSERPINE [*snubbing him*] Talk about indifferent things. Talk about the weather.

MARCHBANKS. Would you stand and talk about indifferent things if a child were by, crying bitterly with hunger?

PROSERPINE. I suppose not.

MARCHBANKS. Well : *I* cant talk about indifferent things with my heart crying out bitterly in its hunger.

PROSERPINE. Then hold your tongue.

MARCHBANKS. Yes : that is what it always comes to. We hold our tongues. Does that stop the cry of your heart? — for it does cry: doesnt it? It must, if you have a heart.

PROSERPINE [*suddenly rising with her hand pressed on her heart*] Oh, it's no use trying to work while you talk like that. [*She leaves her little table and sits on the sofa. Her feelings are keenly stirred*]. It's no business of yours whether my heart cries or not; but I have a mind to tell you, for all that.

MARCHBANKS. You neednt. I know already that it must.

PROSERPINE. But mind : if you ever say I said so, I'll deny it.

MARCHBANKS [*compassionately*] Yes, I know. And so you havnt the courage to tell him?

PROSERPINE [*bouncing up*] Him! Who?

MARCHBANKS. Whoever he is. The man you love. It might be anybody. The curate, Mr Mill, perhaps.

PROSERPINE [*with disdain*] Mr Mill !!! A fine man to break my heart about, indeed ! I'd rather have you than Mr Mill.

MARCHBANKS [*recoiling*] No, really : I'm very sorry ; but you musnt think of that. I—

PROSERPINE [*testily, crossing to the fire and standing at it with her back to him*] Oh, dont be frightened : it's not you. It's not any one particular person.

MARCHBANKS. I know. You feel that you could love anybody that offered—

PROSERPINE [*exasperated*] Anybody that offered ! No, I do not. What do you take me for?

MARCHBANKS [*discouraged*] No use. You wont make me
real answers — only those things that everybody says.
[*He strays to the sofa and sits down disconsolately*].

PROSERPINE [*nettled at what she takes to be a disparagement of her manners by an aristocrat*] Oh, well, if you
want original conversation, youd better go and talk to yourself.

MARCHBANKS. That is what all poets do : they talk to
themselves out loud ; and the world overhears them.
But it's horribly lonely not to hear someone else talk sometimes.

PROSERPINE. Wait until Mr Morell comes. He'll
talk to you. [*Marchbanks shudders*]. Oh, you neednt make
wry faces over him : he can talk better than you. [*With
temper*] He'd talk your little head off. [*She is going back
angrily to her place, when he, suddenly enlightened, springs up
and stops her*].

MARCHBANKS. Ah, I understand now !

PROSERPINE [*reddening*] What do you understand ?

MARCHBANKS. Your secret. Tell me : is it really and
truly possible for a woman to love him ?

PROSERPINE [*as if this were beyond all bounds*] Well ! !

MARCHBANKS [*passionately*] No, answer me. I want to
know : I must know. *I* cant understand it. I can see
nothing in him but words, pious resolutions, what people
call goodness. You cant love that.

PROSERPINE [*attempting to snub him by an air of cool pro-
priety*] I simply dont know what youre talking about. I
dont understand you.

MARCHBANKS [*vehemently*] You do. You lie :—

PROSERPINE. Oh !

MARCHBANKS. —you do understand ; and you know.
[*Determined to have an answer*] Is it possible for a woman
to love him ?

PROSERPINE [*looking him straight in the face*] Yes. [*He
covers his face with his hands*]. Whatever is the matter with
you ! [*He takes down his hands and looks at her. Frightened*

*at the tragic mask presented to her, she hurries past him at the
utmost possible distance, keeping her eyes on his face until he
turns from her and goes to the child's chair beside the hearth,
where he sits in the deepest dejection. As she approaches the
door, it opens and Burgess enters. On seeing him, she ejacu-
lates]* Praise heaven, here's somebody! *[and sits down, re-
assured, at her table. She puts a fresh sheet of paper into the
typewriter as Burgess crosses to Eugene].*

BURGESS *[bent on taking care of the distinguished visitor]*
Well : so this is the way they leave you to yoreself, Mr
Morchbanks. Ive come to keep you company. *[March-
banks looks up at him in consternation, which is quite lost on
him].* James is receivin a deppitation in the dinin room ;
and Candy is hupstairs educatin of a young stitcher gurl
she's hinterusted in. She's settin there learnin her to read
out of the " Evnly Twins." *[Condolingly]* You must find
it lonesome here with no one but the typist to talk to.
[He pulls round the easy chair, and sits down].

PROSERPINE *[highly incensed]* He'll be all right now that
he has the advantage of your polished conversation :
thats one comfort, anyhow. *[She begins to typewrite with
clattering asperity].*

BURGESS *[amazed at her audacity]* Hi was not addressin
myself to you, young woman, that I'm awerr of.

PROSERPINE *[tartly, to Marchbanks]* Did you ever see
worse manners, Mr Marchbanks ?

BURGESS *[with pompous severity]* Mr Morchbanks is a
gentleman, and knows his place, which is more than some
people do.

PROSERPINE *[fretfully]* It's well you and I are not ladies
and gentlemen : I'd talk to you pretty straight if Mr
Marchbanks wasnt here. *[She pulls the letter out of the
machine so crossly that it tears].* There ! now I've spoiled
this letter — have to be done all over again. Oh, I cant
contain myself — silly old fathead !

BURGESS *[rising, breathless with indignation]* Ho ! I'm a
silly ole fat'ead, am I ? Ho, indeed *[gasping]*! Hall right,

my gurl! Hall right. You just wait till I tell that to yore hemployer. Youll see. I'll teach you : see if I dont.

PROSERPINE. I—

BURGESS [*cutting her short*] No : youve done it now. No huse a-talkin to me. I'll let you know who I am. [*Proserpine shifts her paper carriage with a defiant bang, and disdainfully goes on with her work*]. Dont you take no notice of her, Mr Morchbanks. She's beneath it. [*He loftily sits down again*].

MARCHBANKS [*miserably nervous and disconcerted*] Hadnt we better change the subject? I — I dont think Miss Garnett meant anything.

PROSERPINE [*with intense conviction*] Oh, didnt I though, just!

BURGESS. I wouldnt demean myself to take notice on her. *An electric bell rings twice.*

PROSERPINE [*gathering up her note-book and papers*] Thats for me. [*She hurries out*].

BURGESS [*calling after her*] Oh, we can spare you. [*Somewhat relieved by the triumph of having the last word, and yet half inclined to try to improve on it, he looks after her for a moment; then subsides into his seat by Eugene, and addresses him very confidentially*]. Now we're alone, Mr Morchbanks, let me give you a friendly int that I wouldnt give to heverybody. Ow long ave you known my son-in-law James ere?

MARCHBANKS. I dont know. I never can remember dates. A few months, perhaps.

BURGESS. Ever notice hennythink queer about him?

MARCHBANKS. I dont think so.

BURGESS [*impressively*] No more you wouldnt. Thats the danger in it. Well, he's mad.

MARCHBANKS. Mad!

BURGESS. Mad as a Morch 'are. You take notice on him and youll see.

MARCHBANKS [*uneasily*] But surely that is only because his opinions—

BURGESS [*touching him on the knee with his forefinger, and pressing it to hold his attention*] Thats the same what I hused to think, Mr Morchbanks. Hi thought long enough that it was ony his opinions ; though, mind you, hopinions becomes vurry serious things when people takes to hactin on em as e does. But thats not what I go on. [*He looks round to make sure that they are alone, and bends over to Eugene's ear*]. What do you think he sez to me this mornin in this very room ?

MARCHBANKS. What ?

BURGESS. He sez to me — this is as sure as we're settin here now — he sez : "I'm a fool," he sez ; "and yore a scounderl " — as cool as possible. Me a scounderl, mind you ! And then shook ands with me on it, as if it was to my credit ! Do you mean to tell me that that man's sane ?

MORELL [*outside, calling to Proserpine, as he opens the door*] Get all their names and addresses, Miss Garnett.

PROSERPINE [*in the distance*] Yes, Mr Morell.

Morell comes in, with the deputation's documents in his hands.

BURGESS [*aside to Marchbanks*] Yorr he is. Just you keep your heye on im and see. [*Rising momentously*] I'm sorry, James, to ave to make a complaint to you. I dont want to do it ; but I feel I oughter, as a matter o right and dooty.

MORELL. Whats the matter ?

BURGESS. Mr Morchbanks will bear me hout : he was a witness. [*Very solemnly*] Yore young woman so far forgot herself as to call me a silly ole fat'ead.

MORELL [*with tremendous heartiness*] Oh, now, isnt that exactly like Prossy ? She's so frank : she cant contain herself ! Poor Prossy ! Ha ! ha !

BURGESS [*trembling with rage*] And do you hexpec me to put up with it from the like of er ?

MORELL. Pooh, nonsense ! you cant take any notice of it. Never mind. [*He goes to the cellaret and puts the papers into one of the drawers*].

BURGESS. Oh, Hi dont mind. Hi'm above it. But is it right? thats what I want to know. Is it right?

MORELL. Thats a question for the Church, not for the laity. Has it done you any harm? thats the question for you, eh? Of course it hasnt. Think no more of it. [*He dismisses the subject by going to his place at the table and setting to work at his correspondence*].

BURGESS [*aside to Marchbanks*] What did I tell you? Mad as a atter. [*He goes to the table and asks, with the sickly civility of a hungry man*] When's dinner, James?

MORELL. Not for a couple of hours yet.

BURGESS [*with plaintive resignation*] Gimme a nice book to read over the fire, will you, James : thur's a good chap.

MORELL. What sort of book? A good one?

BURGESS [*with almost a yell of remonstrance*] Nah-oo! Summat pleasant, just to pass the time. [*Morell takes an illustrated paper from the table and offers it. He accepts it humbly*]. Thank yer, James. [*He goes back to the big chair at the fire, and sits there at his ease, reading*].

MORELL [*as he writes*] Candida will come to entertain you presently. She has got rid of her pupil. She is filling the lamps.

MARCHBANKS [*starting up in the wildest consternation*] But that will soil her hands. I cant bear that, Morell : it's a shame. I'll go and fill them. [*He makes for the door*].

MORELL. Youd better not. [*Marchbanks stops irresolutely*]. Shed only set you to clean my boots, to save me the trouble of doing it myself in the morning.

BURGESS [*with grave disapproval*] Dont you keep a servant now, James?

MORELL. Yes ; but she isnt a slave ; and the house looks as if I kept three. That means that everyone has to lend a hand. It's not a bad plan : Prossy and I can talk business after breakfast whilst we're washing up. Washing up's no trouble when there are two people to do it.

MARCHBANKS [*tormentedly*] Do you think every woman is as coarse-grained as Miss Garnett?

BURGESS [*emphatically*] Thats quite right, Mr Morchbanks : thats quite right. She is corse-grained.

MORELL [*quietly and significantly*] Marchbanks !

MARCHBANKS. Yes.

MORELL. How many servants does your father keep ?

MARCHBANKS. Oh, I dont know. [*He comes back uneasily to the sofa, as if to get as far as possible from Morell's questioning, and sits down in great agony of mind, thinking of the paraffin*].

MORELL [*very gravely*] So many that you dont know ! [*More aggressively*] Anyhow, when theres anything coarse-grained to be done, you ring the bell and throw it on to somebody else, eh ? Thats one of the great facts in your existence, isnt it ?

MARCHBANKS. Oh, dont torture me. The one great fact now is that your wife's beautiful fingers are dabbling in paraffin oil, and that you are sitting here comfortably preaching about it — everlasting preaching, preaching, words ! words ! words !

BURGESS [*intensely appreciating this retort*] Har, har ! Devil a better ! [*Radiantly*] Ad you there, James, straight.

Candida comes in, well aproned, with a reading lamp trimmed, filled, and ready for lighting. She places it on the table near Morell, ready for use.

CANDIDA [*brushing her finger tips together with a slight twitch of her nose*] If you stay with us, Eugene, I think I will hand over the lamps to you.

MARCHBANKS. I will stay on condition that you hand over all the rough work to me.

CANDIDA. Thats very gallant ; but I think I should like to see how you do it first. [*Turning to Morell*] James : youve not been looking after the house properly.

MORELL. What have I done — or not done — my love ?

CANDIDA [*with serious vexation*] My own particular pet scrubbing brush has been used for blackleading. [*A heart-breaking wail bursts from Marchbanks. Burgess looks round, amazed. Candida hurries to the sofa*]. Whats the matter ? Are you ill, Eugene ?

Burgess, not deigning to reply, strikes an attitude of the haughtiest disdain on the hearth-rug.

PROSERPINE [*calmly*] I should never have supposed you had it in you. By the way, I'd better warn you, since youve taken such a fancy to Mr Marchbanks. He's mad.

BURGESS. Mad! What! Im too!!

PROSERPINE. Mad as a March hare. He did frighten me, I can tell you, just before you came in that time. Havnt you noticed the queer things he says?

BURGESS. So thats what the poetic orrors means. Blame me if it didnt come into my head once or twyst that he must be horff 'is chump! [*He crosses the room to the door, lifting up his voice as he goes*]. Well, this is a pretty sort of asylum for a man to be in, with no one but you to take care of him!

PROSERPINE [*as he passes her*] Yes, what a dreadful thing it would be if anything happened to you!

BURGESS [*loftily*] Dont you haddress no remorks to me. Tell your hemployer that Ive gone into the gawrden for a smoke.

PROSERPINE [*mocking*] Oh!

Before Burgess can retort, Morell comes back.

BURGESS [*sentimentally*] Goin for a turn in the gawrding to smoke, James.

MORELL [*brusquely*] Oh, all right, all right. [*Burgess goes out pathetically in the character of a weary old man. Morell stands at the table, turning over his papers, and adding, across to Proserpine, half humorously, half absently*] Well, Miss Prossy, why have you been calling my father-in-law names?

PROSERPINE [*blushing fiery red, and looking quickly up at him, half scared, half reproachful*] I— [*She bursts into tears*].

MORELL [*with tender gaiety, leaning across the table towards her, and consoling her*] Oh, come, come, come! Never mind, Pross: he is a silly old fathead, isnt he?

With an explosive sob, she makes a dash at the door, and vanishes, banging it. Morell, shaking his head resignedly, sighs,

*and goes wearily to his chair, where he sits down and sets
to work, looking old and careworn.*

*Candida comes in. She has finished her household work ana
taken off the apron. She at once notices his dejected appearance, and posts herself quietly at the visitors' chair, looking down
at him attentively. She says nothing.*

MORELL [*looking up, but with his pen raised ready to resume
his work*] Well? Where is Eugene?

CANDIDA. Washing his hands in the scullery — under
the tap. He will make an excellent cook if he can only
get over his dread of Maria.

MORELL [*shortly*] Ha! No doubt. [*He begins writing
again*].

CANDIDA [*going nearer, and putting her hand down softly
on his to stop him, as she says*] Come here, dear. Let me look
at you. [*He drops his pen and yields himself to her disposal.
She makes him rise, and brings him a little away from the
table, looking at him critically all the time*]. Turn your face to
the light. [*She places him facing the window*]. My boy is
not looking well. Has he been overworking?

MORELL. Nothing more than usual.

CANDIDA. He looks very pale, and grey, and wrinkled,
and old. [*His melancholy deepens; and she attacks it with
wilful gaiety*] Here: [*pulling him towards the easy chair*]
youve done enough writing for to-day. Leave Prossy to
finish it and come and talk to me.

MORELL. But—

CANDIDA [*insisting*] Yes, I must be talked to. [*She
makes him sit down, and seats herself on the carpet beside his
knee*]. Now [*patting his hand*] youre beginning to look
better already. Why dont you give up all this tiresome
overworking — going out every night lecturing and talking?
Of course what you say is all very true and very right; but
it does no good: they dont mind what you say to them
one little bit. Of course they agree with you; but whats
the use of people agreeing with you if they go and do just
the opposite of what you tell them the moment your back

MORELL [*grimly*] Oh, he has no suspicion of it himself, hasnt he ?

CANDIDA. Not a bit. [*She takes her arms from his knee, and turns thoughtfully, sinking into a more restful attitude with her hands in her lap*]. Some day he will know — when he is grown up and experienced, like you. And he will know that I must have known. I wonder what he will think of me then.

MORELL. No evil, Candida. I hope and trust, no evil.

CANDIDA [*dubiously*] That will depend.

MORELL [*bewildered*] Depend !

CANDIDA [*looking at him*] Yes : it will depend on what happens to him. [*He looks vacantly at her*]. Dont you see ? It will depend on how he comes to learn what love really is. I mean on the sort of woman who will teach it to him.

MORELL [*quite at a loss*] Yes. No. I dont know what you mean.

CANDIDA [*explaining*] If he learns it from a good woman, then it will be all right : he will forgive me.

MORELL. Forgive !

CANDIDA. But suppose he learns it from a bad woman, as so many men do, especially poetic men, who imagine all women are angels ! Suppose he only discovers the value of love when he has thrown it away and degraded himself in his ignorance ! Will he forgive me then, do you think ?

MORELL. Forgive you for what ?

CANDIDA [*realizing how stupid he is, and a little disappointed, though quite tenderly so*] Dont you understand ? [*He shakes his head. She turns to him again, so as to explain with the fondest intimacy*]. I mean, will he forgive me for not teaching him myself ? For abandoning him to the bad women for the sake of my goodness — my purity, as you call it ? Ah, James, how little you understand me, to talk of your confidence in my goodness and purity ! I would give them both to poor Eugene as willingly as I would give my shawl to a beggar dying of cold, if there

were nothing else to restrain me. Put your trust in my
love for you, James; for if that went, I should care very
little for your sermons — mere phrases that you cheat
yourself and others with every day. [*She is about to
rise*].

MORELL. His words!

CANDIDA [*checking herself quickly in the act of getting up*]
Whose words?

MORELL. Eugene's.

CANDIDA [*delighted*] He is always right. He understands you; he understands me; he understands Prossy;
and you, James! you understand nothing. [*She laughs,
and kisses him to console him. He recoils as if stabbed, and
springs up*].

MORELL. How can you bear to do that when — oh,
Candida [*with anguish in his voice*] I had rather you had
plunged a grappling iron into my heart than given me that
kiss.

CANDIDA [*rising, alarmed*] My dear: whats the matter?

MORELL [*frantically waving her off*] Dont touch me.

CANDIDA [*amazed*] James!

*They are interrupted by the entrance of Marchbanks, with
Burgess, who stops near the door, staring, whilst Eugene hurries
forward between them.*

MARCHBANKS. Is anything the matter?

MORELL [*deadly white, putting an iron constraint on himself*]
Nothing but this: that either you were right this morning,
or Candida is mad.

BURGESS [*in loudest protest*] What! Candy mad too!
Oh, come, come, come! [*He crosses the room to the fireplace, protesting as he goes, and knocks the ashes out of his pipe
on the bars. Morell sits down desperately, leaning forward to
hide his face, and interlacing his fingers rigidly to keep them
steady*].

CANDIDA [*to Morell, relieved and laughing*] Oh, youre
only shocked! Is that all? How conventional all you
unconventional people are!

BURGESS. Come : be'ave yourself, Candy. Whatll Mr Morchbanks think of you ?

CANDIDA. This comes of James teaching me to think for myself, and never to hold back out of fear of what other people may think of me. It works beautifully as long as I think the same things as he docs. But now ! because I have just thought something different ! — look at him ! just look ! [*She points to Morell, greatly amused. Eugene looks, and instantly presses his hand on his heart, as if some pain had shot through it. He sits down on the sofa like a man witnessing a tragedy*].

BURGESS [*on the hearth-rug*] Well, James, you certnly aint as himpressive lookin as usu'l.

MORELL [*with a laugh which is half a sob*] I suppose not. I beg all your pardons : I was not conscious of making a fuss. [*Pulling himself together*] Well, well, well, well, well ! [*He goes back to his place at the table, setting to work at his papers again with resolute cheerfulness*].

CANDIDA [*going to the sofa and sitting beside Marchbanks, still in a bantering humor*] Well, Eugene : why are you so sad ? Did the onions make you cry ?

Morell cannot prevent himself from watching them.

MARCHBANKS [*aside to her*] It is your cruelty. I hate cruelty. It is a horrible thing to see one person make another suffer.

CANDIDA [*petting him ironically*] Poor boy ! have I been cruel ? Did I make it slice nasty little red onions ?

MARCHBANKS [*earnestly*] Oh, stop, stop : I dont mean myself. You have made him suffer frightfully. I feel his pain in my own heart. I know that it is not your fault — it is something that must happen ; but dont make light of it. I shudder when you torture him and laugh.

CANDIDA [*incredulously*] *I* torture James ! Nonsense, Eugene : how you exaggerate ! Silly ! [*She looks round at Morell, who hastily resumes his writing. She goes to him and stands behind his chair, bending over him*]. Dont work any more, dear. Come and talk to us.

MORELL [*affectionately but bitterly*] Ah no : *I* cant talk. I can only preach.

CANDIDA [*caressing him*] Well, come and preach.

BURGESS [*strongly remonstrating*] Aw no, Candy. 'Ang it all !

Lexy Mill comes in, looking anxious and important.

LEXY [*hastening to shake hands with Candida*] How do you do, Mrs Morell ?   So glad to see you back again.

CANDIDA. Thank you, Lexy.   You know Eugene, dont you ?

LEXY. Oh yes.   How do you do, Marchbanks ?

MARCHBANKS. Quite well, thanks.

LEXY [*to Morell*] Ive just come from the Guild of St Matthew.   They are in the greatest consternation about your telegram.   Theres nothing wrong, is there ?

CANDIDA. What did you telegraph about, James ?

LEXY [*to Candida*] He was to have spoken for them to-night.   Theyve taken the large hall in Mare Street and spent a lot of money on posters.   Morell's telegram was to say he couldnt come.   It came on them like a thunderbolt.

CANDIDA [*surprised, and beginning to suspect something wrong*] Given up an engagement to speak !

BURGESS. Fust time in his life, I'll bet.   Ain it, Candy ?

LEXY [*to Morell*] They decided to send an urgent telegram to you asking whether you could not change your mind.   Have you received it ?

MORELL [*with restrained impatience*] Yes, yes : I got it.

LEXY. It was reply paid.

MORELL. Yes, I know.   I answered it.   I cant go.

CANDIDA. But why, James ?

MORELL [*almost fiercely*] Because I dont choose.   These people forget that I am a man : they think I am a talking machine to be turned on for their pleasure every evening of my life.   May I not have one night at home, with my wife, and my friends ?

They are all amazed at this outburst, except Eugene. His expression remains unchanged.

CANDIDA. Oh, James, you know youll have an attack of bad conscience to-morrow; and *I* shall have to suffer for that.

LEXY [*intimidated, but urgent*] I know, of course, that they make the most unreasonable demands on you. But they have been telegraphing all over the place for another speaker; and they can get nobody but the President of the Agnostic League.

MORELL [*promptly*] Well, an excellent man. What better do they want?

LEXY. But he always insists so powerfully on the divorce of Socialism from Christianity. He will undo all the good we have been doing. Of course you know best; but— [*he hesitates*].

CANDIDA [*coaxingly*] Oh, do go, James. We'll all go.

BURGESS [*grumbling*] Look 'ere, Candy! I say! Let's stay at home by the fire, comfortable. He wont need to be more'n a couple-o-hour away.

CANDIDA. Youll be just as comfortable at the meeting. We'll all sit on the platform and be great people.

EUGENE [*terrified*] Oh please dont let us go on the platform. No: everyone will stare at us: I couldnt. I'll sit at the back of the room.

CANDIDA. Dont be afraid. Theyll be too busy looking at James to notice you.

MORELL [*turning his head to look meaningly at her over his shoulder*] Prossy's complaint, Candida! Eh?

CANDIDA [*gaily*] Yes.

BURGESS [*mystified*] Prossy's complaint! What are you talkin about, James?

MORELL [*not heeding him, rises; goes to the door; and holds it open, calling in a commanding tone*] Miss Garnett.

PROSERPINE [*in the distance*] Yes, Mr Morell. Coming.

They all wait, except Burgess, who goes stealthily to Lexy and draws him aside.

BURGESS. Listen ere, Mr Mill. Whats Prossy's complaint? Whats wrong with er?

LEXY [*confidentially*] Well, I dont exactly know ; but she spoke very strangely to me this morning. I'm afraid she's a little out of her mind sometimes.

BURGESS [*overwhelmed*] Why, it must be catchin ! Four in the same ouse ! [*He goes back to the hearth, quite lost before the instability of the human intellect in a clerical atmosphere*].

PROSERPINE [*appearing on the threshold*] What is it, Mr Morell ?

MORELL. Telegraph to the Guild of St Matthew that I am coming.

PROSERPINE [*surprised*] Dont they expect you ?

MORELL [*peremptorily*] Do as I tell you.

Proserpine, frightened, sits down at her typewriter, and obeys. Morell goes across to Burgess, Candida watching his movements all the time with growing wonder and misgiving.

MORELL. Burgess : you dont want to come ?

BURGESS [*in deprecation*] Oh, dont put it like that, James. It's ony that it aint Sunday, you know.

MORELL. I'm sorry. I thought you might like to be introduced to the chairman. He's on the Works Committee of the County Council, and has some influence in the matter of contracts. [*Burgess wakes up at once. Morell, expecting as much, waits a moment, and says*] Will you come ?

BURGESS [*with enthusiasm*] Cawrse I'll come, James. Ain' it awlus a pleasure to ear you !

MORELL [*turning to Prossy*] I shall want you to take some notes at the meeting, Miss Garnett, if you have no other engagement. [*She nods, afraid to speak*]. You are coming, Lexy, I suppose ?

LEXY. Certainly.

CANDIDA. We're all coming, James.

MORELL. No : you are not coming ; and Eugene is not coming. You will stay here and entertain him — to celebrate your return home. [*Eugene rises, breathless*].

CANDIDA. But, James—

MORELL [*authoritatively*] I insist. You do not want to

come ; and he does not want to come. [*Candida is about to protest*]. Oh, dont concern yourselves : I shall have plenty of people without you : your chairs will be wanted by unconverted people who have never heard me before.

CANDIDA [*troubled*] Eugene : wouldnt you like to come ?

MORELL. I should be afraid to let myself go before Eugene : he is so critical of sermons. [*Looking at him*] He knows I am afraid of him : he told me as much this morning. Well, I shall shew him how much afraid I am by leaving him here in your custody, Candida.

MARCHBANKS [*to himself, with vivid feeling*] Thats brave. Thats beautiful. [*He sits down again, listening with parted lips*].

CANDIDA [*with anxious misgiving*] But — but— Is anything the matter, James ? [*Greatly troubled*] I cant understand—

MORELL. Ah, I thought it was *I* who couldnt understand, dear. [*He takes her tenderly in his arms and kisses her on the forehead ; then looks round quietly at Marchbanks*].

ACT III

Past ten in the evening. The curtains are drawn, and the lamps lighted. The typewriter is in its case: the large table has been cleared and tidied: everything indicates that the day's work is over.

Candida and Marchbanks are sitting by the fire. The reading lamp is on the mantelshelf above Marchbanks, who is in the small chair, reading aloud. A little pile of manuscripts and a couple of volumes of poetry are on the carpet beside him. Candida is in the easy chair. The poker, a light brass one, is upright in her hand. Leaning back and looking at the point of it curiously, with her feet stretched towards the blaze and her heels resting on the fender, she is profoundly unconscious of her appearance and surroundings.

MARCHBANKS [*breaking off in his recitation*] Every poet that ever lived has put that thought into a sonnet. He must: he cant help it. [*He looks to her for assent, and notices her absorption in the poker*]. Havnt you been listening? [*No response*]. Mrs Morell!

CANDIDA [*starting*] Eh?

MARCHBANKS. Havnt you been listening?

CANDIDA [*with a guilty excess of politeness*] Oh yes. It's very nice. Go on, Eugene. I'm longing to hear what happens to the angel.

MARCHBANKS [*letting the manuscript drop from his hand to the floor*] I beg your pardon for boring you.

CANDIDA. But you are not boring me, I assure you. Please go on. Do, Eugene.

MARCHBANKS. I finished the poem about the angel quarter of an hour ago. Ive read you several things since.

CANDIDA [*remorsefully*] I'm so sorry, Eugene. I think the poker must have fascinated me. [*She puts it down*].

MARCHBANKS. It made me horribly uneasy.

CANDIDA. Why didnt you tell me? I'd have put it down at once.

MARCHBANKS. I was afraid of making you uneasy too. It looked as if it were a weapon. If I were a hero of old I should have laid my drawn sword between us. If Morell had come in he would have thought you had taken up the poker because there was no sword between us.

CANDIDA [*wondering*] What? [*With a puzzled glance at him*] I cant quite follow that. Those sonnets of yours have perfectly addled me. Why should there be a sword between us?

MARCHBANKS [*evasively*] Oh, never mind. [*He stoops to pick up the manuscript*].

CANDIDA. Put that down again, Eugene. There are limits to my appetite for poetry — even your poetry. Youve been reading to me for more than two hours — ever since James went out. I want to talk.

MARCHBANKS [*rising, scared*] No: I musnt talk. [*He looks round him in his lost way, and adds, suddenly*] I think I'll go out and take a walk in the park. [*He makes for the door*].

CANDIDA. Nonsense: it's shut long ago. Come and sit down on the hearth-rug, and talk moonshine as you usually do. I want to be amused. Dont you want to?

MARCHBANKS [*half in terror, half enraptured*] Yes.

CANDIDA. Then come along. [*She moves her chair back a little to make room. He hesitates; then timidly stretches himself on the hearth-rug, face upwards, and throws back his head across her knees, looking up at her*].

MARCHBANKS. Oh, Ive been so miserable all the evening, because I was doing right. Now I'm doing wrong; and I'm happy.

CANDIDA [*tenderly amused at him*] Yes : I'm sure you feel a great grown-up wicked deceiver — quite proud of yourself, arnt you ?

MARCHBANKS [*raising his head quickly and turning a little to look round at her*] Take care. I'm ever so much older than you, if you only knew. [*He turns quite over on his knees, with his hands clasped and his arms on her lap, and speaks with growing impulse, his blood beginning to stir*]. May I say some wicked things to you ?

CANDIDA [*without the least fear or coldness, and with perfect respect for his passion, but with a touch of her wise-hearted maternal humor*] No. But you may say anything you really and truly feel. Anything at all, no matter what it is. I am not afraid, so long as it is your real self that speaks, and not a mere attitude — a gallant attitude, or a wicked attitude, or even a poetic attitude. I put you on your honor and truth. Now say whatever you want to.

MARCHBANKS [*the eager expression vanishing utterly from his lips and nostrils as his eyes light up with pathetic spirituality*] Oh, now I cant say anything : all the words I know belong to some attitude or other — all except one.

CANDIDA. What one is that ?

MARCHBANKS [*softly, losing himself in the music of the name*] Candida, Candida, Candida, Candida, Candida. I must say that now, because you have put me on my honor and truth ; and I never think or feel Mrs Morell : it is always Candida.

CANDIDA. Of course. And what have you to say to Candida ?

MARCHBANKS. Nothing but to repeat your name a thousand times. Dont you feel that every time is a prayer to you ?

CANDIDA. Doesnt it make you happy to be able to pray ?

MARCHBANKS. Yes, very happy.

CANDIDA. Well, that happiness is the answer to your prayer. Do you want anything more ?

MARCHBANKS [*in beatitude*] No : I have come into heaven, where want is unknown.

Morell comes in. He halts on the threshold, and takes in the scene at a glance.

MORELL [*grave and self-contained*] I hope I dont disturb you.

Candida starts up violently, but without the smallest embarrassment, laughing at herself. Eugene, still kneeling, saves himself from falling by putting his hands on the seat of the chair, and remains there, staring open-mouthed at Morell.

CANDIDA [*as she rises*] Oh, James, how you startled me ! I was so taken up with Eugene that I didnt hear your latch-key. How did the meeting go off ? Did you speak well ?

MORELL. I have never spoken better in my life.

CANDIDA. That was first rate ! How much was the collection ?

MORELL. I forgot to ask.

CANDIDA [*to Eugene*] He must have spoken splendidly, or he would never have forgotten that. [*To Morell*]. Where are all the others ?

MORELL. They left long before I could get away : I thought I should never escape. I believe they are having supper somewhere.

CANDIDA [*in her domestic business tone*] Oh, in that case, Maria may go to bed. I'll tell her. [*She goes out to the kitchen*].

MORELL [*looking sternly down at Marchbanks*] Well ?

MARCHBANKS [*squatting cross-legged on the hearth-rug, and actually at ease with Morell — even impishly humorous*] Well ?

MORELL. Have you anything to tell me ?

MARCHBANKS. Only that I have been making a fool of myself here in private whilst you have been making a fool of yourself in public.

MORELL. Hardly in the same way, I think.

MARCHBANKS [*eagerly, scrambling up*] The very, very, very same way. I have been playing the good man just like you. When you began your heroics about leaving me here with Candida—

MORELL [*involuntarily*] Candida !

MARCHBANKS. Oh yes : Ive got that far. Heroics are infectious : I caught the disease from you. I swore not to say a word in your absence that I would not have said a month ago in your presence.

MORELL. Did you keep your oath ?

MARCHBANKS [*suddenly perching himself grotesquely on the easy chair*] I was ass enough to keep it until about ten minutes ago. Up to that moment I went on desperately reading to her — reading my own poems — anybody's poems — to stave off a conversation. I was standing outside the gate of Heaven, and refusing to go in. Oh, you cant think how heroic it was, and how uncomfortable ! Then—

MORELL [*steadily controlling his suspense*] Then ?

MARCHBANKS [*prosaically slipping down into a quite ordinary attitude in the chair*] Then she couldnt bear being read to any longer.

MORELL. And you approached the gate of Heaven at last ?

MARCHBANKS. Yes.

MORELL. Well ? [*Fiercely*] Speak, man : have you no feeling for me ?

MARCHBANKS [*softly and musically*] Then she became an angel ; and there was a flaming sword that turned every way, so that I couldnt go in ; for I saw that that gate was really the gate of Hell.

MORELL [*triumphantly*] She repulsed you !

MARCHBANKS [*rising in wild scorn*] No, you fool : if she had done that I should never have seen that I was in Heaven already. Repulsed me ! You think that would have saved me — virtuous indignation ! Oh, you are not worthy to live in the same world with her. [*He turns away contemptuously to the other side of the room*]

MORELL [*who has watched him quietly without changing his place*] Do you think you make yourself more worthy by reviling me, Eugene ?

MARCHBANKS. Here endeth the thousand and first lesson. Morell : I dont think much of your preaching after all : I believe I could do it better myself. The man I want to meet is the man that Candida married.

MORELL. The man that — ? Do you mean me ?

MARCHBANKS. I dont mean the Reverend James Mavor Morell, moralist and windbag. I mean the real man that the Reverend James must have hidden somewhere inside his black coat — the man that Candida loved. You cant make a woman like Candida love you by merely buttoning your collar at the back instead of in front.

MORELL [*boldly and steadily*] When Candida promised to marry me, I was the same moralist and windbag you now see. I wore my black coat ; and my collar was buttoned behind instead of in front. Do you think she would have loved me any the better for being insincere in my profession ?

MARCHBANKS [*on the sofa, hugging his ankles*] Oh, she forgave you, just as she forgives me for being a coward, and a weakling, and what you call a snivelling little whelp and all the rest of it. [*Dreamily*] A woman like that has divine insight : she loves our souls, and not our follies and vanities and illusions, or our collars and coats, or any other of the rags and tatters we are rolled up in. [*He reflects on this for an instant ; then turns intently to question Morell*]. What I want to know is how you got past the flaming sword that stopped me.

MORELL [*meaningly*] Perhaps because I was not interrupted at the end of ten minutes.

MARCHBANKS [*taken aback*] What !

MORELL. Man can climb to the highest summits ; but he cannot dwell there long.

MARCHBANKS. It's false : there can he dwell for ever, and there only. It's in the other moments that he can find no rest, no sense of the silent glory of life. Where would you have me spend my moments, if not on the summits ?

MORELL. In the scullery, slicing onions and filling lamps.

MARCHBANKS. Or in the pulpit, scrubbing cheap earthenware souls ?

MORELL. Yes, that too. It was there that I earned my golden moment, and the right, in that moment, to ask her to love me. *I* did not take the moment on credit ; nor did I use it to steal another man's happiness.

MARCHBANKS [*rather disgustedly, trotting back towards the fireplace*] I have no doubt you conducted the transaction as honestly as if you were buying a pound of cheese. [*He stops on the brink of the hearth-rug, and adds, thoughtfully, to himself, with his back turned to Morell*] I could only go to her as a beggar.

MORELL [*starting*] A beggar dying of cold ! asking for her shawl !

MARCHBANKS [*turning, surprised*] Thank you for touching up my poetry. Yes, if you like : a beggar dying of cold, asking for her shawl.

MORELL [*excitedly*] And she refused. Shall I tell you why she refused ? I c a n tell you, on her own authority. It was because of—

MARCHBANKS. She didnt refuse.

MORELL. Not !

MARCHBANKS. She offered me all I chose to ask for : her shawl, her wings, the wreath of stars on her head, the lilies in her hand, the crescent moon beneath her feet—

MORELL [*seizing him*] Out with the truth, man: my wife is my wife : I want no more of your poetic fripperies. I know well that if I have lost her love and you have gained it, no law will bind her.

MARCHBANKS [*quaintly, without fear or resistance*] Catch me by the shirt collar, Morell : she will arrange it for me afterwards as she did this morning. [*With quiet rapture*] I shall feel her hands touch me.

MORELL. You young imp, do you know how dangerous it is to say that to me ? Or [*with a sudden misgiving*] has something made you brave ?

MARCHBANKS. I'm not afraid now. I disliked you before : that was why I shrank from your touch. But I saw to-day — when she tortured you — that you love her. Since then I have been your friend : you may strangle me if you like.

MORELL [*releasing him*] Eugene : if that is not a heartless lie — if you have a spark of human feeling left in you — will you tell me what has happened during my absence ?

MARCHBANKS. What happened ! Why, the flaming sword— [*Morell stamps with impatience*]. Well, in plain prose, I loved her so exquisitely that I wanted nothing more than the happiness of being in such love. And before I had time to come down from the highest summits, you came in.

MORELL [*suffering deeply*] So it is still unsettled — still the misery of doubt.

MARCHBANKS. Misery ! I am the happiest of men. I desire nothing now but her happiness. [*In a passion of sentiment*] Oh, Morell, let us both give her up. Why should she have to choose between a wretched little nervous disease like me, and a pig-headed parson like you? Let us go on a pilgrimage, you to the east and I to the west, in search of a worthy lover for her — some beautiful archangel with purple wings—

MORELL. Some fiddlestick ! Oh, if she is mad enough to leave me for you, who will protect her ? Who will help her ? who will work for her ? who will be a father to her children ? [*He sits down distractedly on the sofa, with his elbows on his knees and his head propped on his clenched fists*].

MARCHBANKS [*snapping his fingers wildly*] She does not ask those silly questions. It is she who wants somebody to protect, to help, to work for — somebody to give her children to protect, to help and to work for. Some grown up man who has become as a little child again. Oh, you fool, you fool, you triple fool ! I am the man, Morell : I am the man. [*He dances about excitedly, crying*] You

dont understand what a woman is.   Send for her, Morell :
send for her and let her choose between— [*The door opens
and Candida enters.   He stops as if petrified*].

CANDIDA [*amazed, on the threshold*] What on earth are
you at, Eugene ?

MARCHBANKS [*oddly*] James and I are having a preaching
match ; and he is getting the worst of it.   [*Candida looks
quickly round at Morell.   Seeing that he is distressed, she
hurries down to him, greatly vexed, speaking with vigorous
reproach to Marchbanks*].

CANDIDA. You have been annoying him.   Now I wont
have it, Eugene : do you hear ?   [*She puts her hand on
Morell's shoulder, and quite forgets her wifely tact in her
annoyance*].   My boy shall not be worried : I will protect
him.

MORELL [*rising proudly*] Protect !

CANDIDA [*not heeding him — to Eugene*] What have you
been saying ?

MARCHBANKS [*appalled*] Nothing.   I—

CANDIDA. Eugene !   Nothing ?

MARCHBANKS [*piteously*] I mean — I — I'm very sorry.
I wont do it again : indeed I wont.   I'll let him alone.

MORELL [*indignantly, with an aggressive movement towards
Eugene*] Let me alone !   You young—

CANDIDA [*stopping him*] Sh ! — no : let me deal with
him, James.

MARCHBANKS. Oh, youre not angry with me, are you ?

CANDIDA [*severely*] Yes I am — very angry.   I have a
good mind to pack you out of the house.

MORELL [*taken aback by Candida's vigor, and by no means
relishing the position of being rescued by her from another man*]
Gently, Candida, gently.   I am able to take care of myself.

CANDIDA [*petting him*] Yes, dear : of course you are.
But you musnt be annoyed and made miserable.

MARCHBANKS [*almost in tears, turning to the door*] I'll
go.

CANDIDA. Oh, you neednt go : I cant turn you out at this time of night. [*Vehemently*] Shame on you! For shame !

MARCHBANKS [*desperately*] But what have I done ?

CANDIDA. I know what you have done — as well as if I had been here all the time. Oh, it was unworthy! You are like a child : you cannot hold your tongue.

MARCHBANKS. I would die ten times over sooner than give you a moment's pain.

CANDIDA [*with infinite contempt for this puerility*] Much good your dying would do me !

MORELL. Candida, my dear : this altercation is hardly quite seemly. It is a matter between two men ; and I am the right person to settle it.

CANDIDA. Two men ! Do you call that a man ? [*To Eugene*] You bad boy !

MARCHBANKS [*gathering a whimsically affectionate courage from the scolding*] If I am to be scolded like a boy, I must make a boy's excuse. He began it. And he's bigger than I am.

CANDIDA [*losing confidence a little as her concern for Morell's dignity takes the alarm*] That cant be true. [*To Morell*] You didnt begin it, James, did you ?

MORELL [*contemptuously*] No.

MARCHBANKS [*indignant*] Oh !

MORELL [*to Eugene*] You began it — this morning. [*Candida, instantly connecting this with his mysterious allusion in the afternoon to something told him by Eugene in the morning, looks at him with quick suspicion. Morell proceeds, with the emphasis of offended superiority*] But your other point is true. I am certainly the bigger of the two, and, I hope, the stronger, Candida. So you had better leave the matter in my hands.

CANDIDA [*again soothing him*] Yes, dear; but— [*troubled*] I dont understand about this morning.

MORELL [*gently snubbing her*] You need not understand, my dear.

CANDIDA. But James, I— [*the street bell rings*]. Oh bother! Here they all come. [*She goes out to let them in*].

MARCHBANKS [*running to Morell*] Oh, Morell, isnt it dreadful? She's angry with us : she hates me. What shall I do?

MORELL [*with quaint desperation, clutching himself by the hair*] Eugene : my head is spinning round. I shall begin to laugh presently. [*He walks up and down the middle of the room*].

MARCHBANKS [*following him anxiously*] No, no : she'll think Ive thrown you into hysterics. Dont laugh.

Boisterous voices and laughter are heard approaching. Lexy Mill, his eyes sparkling, and his bearing denoting un-wonted elevation of spirit, enters with Burgess, who is greasy and self-complacent, but has all his wits about him. Miss Garnett, with her smartest hat and jacket on, follows them ; but though her eyes are brighter than before, she is evidently a prey to misgiving. She places herself with her back to her typewriting table, with one hand on it to rest herself, passing the other across her forehead as if she were a little tired and giddy. Marchbanks relapses into shyness and edges away into the corner near the window, where Morell's books are.

LEXY [*exhilaratedly*] Morell : I must congratulate you. [*Grasping his hand*] What a noble, splendid, inspired address you gave us! You surpassed yourself.

BURGESS. So you did, James. It fair kep me awake to the lars' word. Didnt it, Miss Gornett?

PROSERPINE [*worriedly*] Oh, I wasnt minding you : I was trying to make notes. [*She takes out her note-book, and looks at her stenography, which nearly makes her cry*].

MORELL. Did I go too fast, Pross?

PROSERPINE. Much too fast. You know I cant do more than ninety words a minute. [*She relieves her feelings by throwing her note-book angrily beside her machine, ready for use next morning*].

MORELL [*soothingly*] Oh well, well, never mind, never mind, never mind. Have you all had supper?

LEXY. Mr Burgess has been kind enough to give us a really splendid supper at the Belgrave.

BURGESS [*with effusive magnanimity*] Dont mention it, Mr Mill. [*Modestly*] Youre arty welcome to my little treat.

PROSERPINE. We had champagne. I never tasted it before. I feel quite giddy.

MORELL [*surprised*] A champagne supper! That was very handsome. Was it my eloquence that produced all this extravagance?

LEXY [*rhetorically*] Your eloquence, and Mr Burgess's goodness of heart. [*With a fresh burst of exhilaration*] And what a very fine fellow the chairman is, Morell! He came to supper with us.

MORELL [*with long drawn significance, looking at Burgess*] O-o-o-h, the chairman! Now I understand.

Burgess, covering with a deprecatory cough a lively satisfaction with his own diplomatic cunning, retires to the hearth. Lexy folds his arms and leans against the cellaret in a high-spirited attitude. Candida comes in with glasses, lemons, and a jug of hot water on a tray.

CANDIDA. Who will have some lemonade? You know our rules : total abstinence. [*She puts the tray on the table, and takes up the lemon squeezer, looking enquiringly round at them*].

MORELL. No use, dear. Theyve all had champagne. Pross has broken her pledge.

CANDIDA [*to Proserpine*] You dont mean to say youve been drinking champagne!

PROSERPINE [*stubbornly*] Yes I do. I'm only a beer tee-totaller, not a champagne teetotaller. I dont like beer. Are there any letters for me to answer, Mr Morell?

MORELL. No more to-night.

PROSERPINE. Very well. Good-night, everybody.

LEXY [*gallantly*] Had I not better see you home, Miss Garnett?

PROSERPINE. No thank you. I shant trust myself with

anybody to-night. I wish I hadnt taken any of that stuff. [*She walks straight out*].

BURGESS [*indignantly*] Stuff indeed! That gurl dunno what champagne is! Pommery and Greeno at twelve and six a bottle. She took two glasses amost straight horff.

MORELL [*a little anxious about her*] Go and look after her, Lexy.

LEXY [*alarmed*] But if she should really be— Suppose she began to sing in the street, or anything of that sort.

MORELL. Just so: she may. Thats why youd better see her safely home.

CANDIDA. Do, Lexy: theres a good fellow. [*She shakes his hand and pushes him gently to the door*].

LEXY. It's evidently my duty to go. I hope it may not be necessary. Good-night, Mrs Morell. [*To the rest*] Good-night. [*He goes. Candida shuts the door*].

BURGESS. He was gushin with hextra piety hisself arter two sips. People carnt drink like they huseter. [*Dismissing the subject and bustling away from the hearth*] Well, James: it's time to lock up. Mr Morchbanks: shall I ave the pleasure of your company for a bit o the way ome?

MARCHBANKS [*affrightedly*] Yes: I'd better go. [*He hurries across to the door; but Candida places herself before it, barring his way*].

CANDIDA [*with quiet authority*] You sit down. Youre not going yet.

MARCHBANKS [*quailing*] No: I — I didnt mean to. [*He comes back into the room and sits down abjectly on the sofa*].

CANDIDA. Mr Marchbanks will stay the night with us, papa.

BURGESS. Oh well, I'll say good-night. So long, James. [*He shakes hands with Morell, and goes over to Eugene*]. Make em give you a nightlight by your bed, Mr Morchbanks: itll comfort you if you wake up in the night with a touch of that complaint of yores. Good-night.

MARCHBANKS. Thank you : I will. Good-night, Mr Burgess. [*They shake hands. Burgess goes to the door*].

CANDIDA [*intercepting Morell, who is following Burgess*] Stay here, dear : I'll put on papa's coat for him. [*She goes out with Burgess*].

MARCHBANKS. Morell : theres going to be a terrible scene. Arnt you afraid ?

MORELL. Not in the least.

MARCHBANKS. I never envied you your courage before. [*He rises timidly and puts his hand appealingly on Morell's forearm*]. Stand by me, wont you ?

MORELL [*casting him off gently, but resolutely*] Each for himself, Eugene. She must choose between us now. [*He goes to the other side of the room as Candida returns. Eugene sits down again on the sofa like a guilty schoolboy on his best behavior*].

CANDIDA [*between them, addressing Eugene*] Are you sorry ?

MARCHBANKS [*earnestly*] Yes, heartbroken.

CANDIDA. Well, then you are forgiven. Now go off to bed like a good little boy : I want to talk to James about you.

MARCHBANKS [*rising in great consternation*] Oh, I cant do that, Morell. I must be here. I'll not go away. Tell her.

CANDIDA [*her suspicions confirmed*] Tell me what ? [*His eyes avoid hers furtively. She turns and mutely transfers the question to Morell*].

MORELL [*bracing himself for the catastrophe*] I have nothing to tell her, except [*here his voice deepens to a measured and mournful tenderness*] that she is my greatest treasure on earth — if she is really mine.

CANDIDA [*coldly, offended by his yielding to his orator's instinct and treating her as if she were the audience at the Guild of St Matthew*] I am sure Eugene can say no less, if that is all.

MARCHBANKS [*discouraged*] Morell : she's laughing at us.

MORELL [*with a quick touch of temper*] There is nothing to laugh at. Are you laughing at us, Candida ?

CANDIDA [*with quiet anger*] Eugene is very quick-witted, James. I hope I am going to laugh ; but I am not sure that I am not going to be very angry. [*She goes to the fire-place, and stands there leaning with her arm on the mantelpiece, and her foot on the fender, whilst Eugene steals to Morell and plucks him by the sleeve*].

MARCHBANKS [*whispering*] Stop, Morell. Dont let us say anything.

MORELL [*pushing Eugene away without deigning to look at him*] I hope you dont mean that as a threat, Candida.

CANDIDA [*with emphatic warning*] Take care, James. Eugene : I asked you to go. Are you going ?

MORELL [*putting his foot down*] He shall not go. I wish him to remain.

MARCHBANKS. I'll go. I'll do whatever you want. [*He turns to the door*].

CANDIDA. Stop ! [*He obeys*]. Didnt you hear James say he wished you to stay ? James is master here. Dont you know that ?

MARCHBANKS [*flushing with a young poet's rage against tyranny*] By what right is he master ?

CANDIDA [*quietly*] Tell him, James.

MORELL [*taken aback*] My dear : I dont know of any right that makes me master. I assert no such right.

CANDIDA [*with infinite reproach*] You dont know ! Oh James, James ! [*To Eugene, musingly*] I wonder do you understand, Eugene ! No : youre too young. Well, I give you leave to stay — to stay and learn. [*She comes away from the hearth and places herself between them*]. Now James : whats the matter ? Come : tell me.

MARCHBANKS [*whispering tremulously across to him*] Dont.

CANDIDA. Come. Out with it !

MORELL [*slowly*] I meant to prepare your mind carefully, Candida, so as to prevent misunderstanding.

CANDIDA. Yes, dear : I am sure you did. But never mind : I shant misunderstand.

MORELL. Well — er— [*he hesitates, unable to find the long explanation which he supposed to be available*].

CANDIDA. Well ?

MORELL [*baldly*] Eugene declares that you are in love with him.

MARCHBANKS [*frantically*] No, no, no, no, never. I did not, Mrs Morell : it's not true. I said I loved you, and that he didnt. I said that I understood you, and that he couldnt. And it was not after what passed there before the fire that I spoke : it was not, on my word. It was this morning.

CANDIDA [*enlightened*] This morning !

MARCHBANKS. Yes. [*He looks at her, pleading for credence, and then adds simply*] That was what was the matter with my collar.

CANDIDA [*after a pause ; for she does not take in his meaning at once*] His collar ! [*She turns to Morell, shocked*]. Oh, James : did you— [*she stops*] ?

MORELL [*ashamed*] You know, Candida, that I have a temper to struggle with. And he said [*shuddering*] that you despised me in your heart.

CANDIDA [*turning quickly on Eugene*] Did you say that ?

MARCHBANKS [*terrified*] No !

CANDIDA [*severely*] Then James has just told me a falsehood. Is that what you mean ?

MARCHBANKS. No, no : I — I— [*blurting out the explanation desperately*] —it was David's wife. And it wasnt at home : it was when she saw him dancing before all the people.

MORELL [*taking the cue with a debater's adroitness*] Dancing before all the people, Candida ; and thinking he was moving their hearts by his mission when they were only suffering from — Prossy's complaint. [*She is about to protest : he raises his hand to silence her, exclaiming*] Dont try to look indignant, Candida :—

CANDIDA. Try !

MORELL [*continuing*] Eugene was right. As you told me

a few hours after, he is always right. He said nothing
that you did not say far better yourself. He is the poet,
who sees everything; and I am the poor parson, who
understands nothing.

CANDIDA [*remorsefully*] Do you mind what is said by a
foolish boy, because I said something like it again in jest?

MORELL. That foolish boy can speak with the inspiration
of a child and the cunning of a serpent. He has claimed
that you belong to him and not to me ; and, rightly or
wrongly, I have come to fear that it may be true. I will
not go about tortured with doubts and suspicions. I will
not live with you and keep a secret from you. I will not
suffer the intolerable degradation of jealousy. We have
agreed — he and I — that you shall choose between us
now. I await your decision.

CANDIDA [*slowly recoiling a step, her heart hardened by his
rhetoric in spite of the sincere feeling behind it*] Oh! I am to
choose, am I ? I suppose it is quite settled that I must
belong to one or the other.

MORELL [*firmly*] Quite. You must choose definitely.

MARCHBANKS [*anxiously*] Morell : you dont understand.
She means that she belongs to herself.

CANDIDA [*turning on him*] I mean that, and a good deal
more, Master Eugene, as you will both find out presently.
And pray, my lords and masters, what have you to offer for
my choice ? I am up for auction, it seems. What do you
bid, James ?

MORELL [*reproachfully*] Cand— [*He breaks down: his
eyes and throat fill with tears : the orator becomes the wounded
animal*]. I cant speak—

CANDIDA [*impulsively going to him*] Ah, dearest—

MARCHBANKS [*in wild alarm*] Stop : it's not fair. You
musnt show her that you suffer, Morell. I am on the
rack too ; but I am not crying.

MORELL [*rallying all his forces*] Yes : you are right. It
is not for pity that I am bidding. [*He disengages himself
from Candida*].

CANDIDA [*retreating, chilled*] I beg your pardon, James ; I did not mean to touch you. I am waiting to hear your bid.

MORELL [*with proud humility*] I have nothing to offer you but my strength for your defence, my honesty of purpose for your surety, my ability and industry for your livelihood, and my authority and position for your dignity. That is all it becomes a man to offer to a woman.

CANDIDA [*quite quietly*] And you, Eugene ? What do you offer ?

MARCHBANKS. My weakness ! my desolation ! my heart's need !

CANDIDA [*impressed*] Thats a good bid, Eugene. Now I know how to make my choice.

She pauses and looks curiously from one to the other, as if weighing them. Morell, whose lofty confidence has changed into heartbreaking dread at Eugene's bid, loses all power of concealing his anxiety. Eugene, strung to the highest tension, does not move a muscle.

MORELL [*in a suffocated voice — the appeal bursting from the depths of his anguish*] Candida !

MARCHBANKS [*aside, in a flash of contempt*] Coward !

CANDIDA [*significantly*] I give myself to the weaker of the two.

Eugene divines her meaning at once : his face whitens like steel in a furnace.

MORELL [*bowing his head with the calm of collapse*] I accept your sentence, Candida.

CANDIDA. Do you understand, Eugene ?

MARCHBANKS. Oh, I feel I'm lost. He cannot bear the burden.

MORELL [*incredulously, raising his head with prosaic abruptness*] Do you mean me, Candida ?

CANDIDA [*smiling a little*] Let us sit and talk comfortably over it like three friends. [*To Morell*] Sit down, dear. [*Morell takes the chair from the fireside — the children's chair*]. Bring me that chair, Eugene. [*She indicates the easy chair. He fetches it silently, even with something like*

cold strength, and places it next Morell, a little behind him.
She sits down.   He goes to the sofa and sits there, still silent
and inscrutable.   When they are all settled she begins, throwing
a spell of quietness on them by her calm, sane, tender tone].
You remember what you told me about yourself, Eugene :
how nobody has cared for you since your old nurse died :
how those clever, fashionable sisters and successful brothers
of yours were your mother's and father's pets : how miserable you were at Eton : how your father is trying to starve
you into returning to Oxford : how you have had to live
without comfort or welcome or refuge, always lonely, and
nearly always disliked and misunderstood, poor boy !

MARCHBANKS [*faithful to the nobility of his lot*] I had my
books. I had Nature. And at last I met you.

CANDIDA. Never mind that just at present. Now I
want you to look at this other boy here — my boy —
spoiled from his cradle. We go once a fortnight to see his
parents. You should come with us, Eugene, and see the
pictures of the hero of that household. James as a baby !
the most wonderful of all babies. James holding his first
school prize, won at the ripe age of eight ! James as the
captain of his eleven ! James in his first frock coat !
James under all sorts of glorious circumstances ! You
know how strong he is (I hope he didnt hurt you) — how
clever he is — how happy ! [*With deepening gravity*] Ask
James's mother and his three sisters what it cost to save
James the trouble of doing anything but be strong and
clever and happy. Ask me what it costs to be James's
mother and three sisters and wife and mother to his children all in one. Ask Prossy and Maria how troublesome
the house is even when we have no visitors to help us to
slice the onions. Ask the tradesmen who want to worry
James and spoil his beautiful sermons who it is that puts
them off. When there is money to give, he gives it :
when there is money to refuse, I refuse it. I build a
castle of comfort and indulgence and love for him, and
stand sentinel always to keep little vulgar cares out. I

make him master here, though he does not know it, and could not tell you a moment ago how it came to be so. [*With sweet irony*] And when he thought I might go away with you, his only anxiety was — what should become of me ! And to tempt me to stay he offered me [*leaning forward to stroke his hair caressingly at each phrase*] his strength for my defence, his industry for my livelihood, his position for my dignity, his— [*relenting*] ah, I am mixing up your beautiful sentences and spoiling them, am I not, darling ? [*She lays her cheek fondly against his*].

MORELL [*quite overcome, kneeling beside her chair and embracing her with boyish ingenuousness*] It's all true, every word. What I am you have made me with the labor of your hands and the love of your heart. You are my wife, my mother, my sisters : you are the sum of all loving care to me.

CANDIDA [*in his arms, smiling, to Eugene*] Am I your mother and sisters to you, Eugene ?

MARCHBANKS [*rising with a fierce gesture of disgust*] Ah, never. Out, then, into the night with me !

CANDIDA [*rising quickly and intercepting him*] You are not going like that, Eugene ?

MARCHBANKS [*with the ring of a man's voice — no longer a boy's — in the words*] I know the hour when it strikes. I am impatient to do what must be done.

MORELL [*rising from his knee, alarmed*] Candida : dont let him do anything rash.

CANDIDA [*confident, smiling at Eugene*] Oh, there is no fear. He has learnt to live without happiness.

MARCHBANKS. I no longer desire happiness : life is nobler than that. Parson James : I give you my happiness with both hands : I love you because you have filled the heart of the woman I loved. Good-bye. [*He goes towards the door*].

CANDIDA. One last word. [*He stops, but without turning to her*]. How old are you, Eugene ?

MARCHBANKS. As old as the world now. This morning I was eighteen.

CANDIDA [*Going to him, and standing behind him with one hand caressingly on his shoulder*] Eighteen! Will you, for my sake, make a little poem out of the two sentences I am going to say to you? And will you promise to repeat it to yourself whenever you think of me.

MARCHBANKS [*without moving*] Say the sentences.

CANDIDA. When I am thirty, she will be forty-five. When I am sixty, she will be seventy-five.

MARCHBANKS [*turning to her*] In a hundred years, we shall be the same age. But I have a better secret than that in my heart. Let me go now. The night outside grows impatient.

CANDIDA. Good-bye. [*She takes his face in her hands; and as he divines her intention and bends his knee, she kisses his forehead. Then he flies out into the night. She turns to Morell, holding out her arms to him*]. Ah, James! [*They embrace. But they do not know the secret in the poet's heart*].

WORKS BY THE SAME AUTHOR.

NOVELS OF MY NONAGE.

No. 1. IMMATURITY (1879). Unpublished.

No. 2. THE IRRATIONAL KNOT (1880). Reprinted with a Preface in 1905. 12s. and 3s. 6d. net.

No. 3. LOVE AMONG THE ARTISTS (1881). 3s. 6d. net.

No. 4. CASHEL BYRON'S PROFESSION (1882), with the dramatic version in the Elizabethan style entitled the ADMIRABLE BASHVILLE or CONSTANCY UNREWARDED, and a Note on Modern Prize-Fighting. 7s. 6d. net and 3s. 6d. net.

No. 5. AN UNSOCIAL SOCIALIST (1883). 3s. 6d. net.

DRAMATIC WORKS.

TRANSLATIONS AND TOMFOOLERIES. Cr. 8vo. 6s. net.
Jitta's Atonement. The Admirable Bashville; or Constancy Unrewarded. Press Cuttings. The Glimpse of Reality. Passion, Poison, and Petrification; or The Fatal Gazogene. The Fascinating Foundling. The Music Cure.

SAINT JOAN. A Chronicle Play. Cr. 8vo. 6s. net

BACK TO METHUSELAH. Cr. 8vo. 10s. net.
PREFACE— IN THE BEGINNING: B.C. 4004 (In the Garden of Eden)— THE GOSPEL OF THE BROTHERS BARNABAS: Present Day— THE THING HAPPENS: A.D. 2170— TRAGEDY OF AN ELDERLY GENTLEMAN: A.D. 3000—As FAR AS THOUGHT CAN REACH: A.D. 31,920.

HEARTBREAK HOUSE, GREAT CATHERINE, AND PLAYLETS OF THE WAR. Cr. 8vo. 7s. 6d. net. PREFACE. HEARTBREAK HOUSE: A Fantasia in the Russian Manner on English Themes—GREAT CATHERINE (Whom Glory still adores)—O'FLAHERTY V.C.: A Recruiting Pamphlet—THE INCA OF PERUSALEM: An Almost Historical Comedietta—AUGUSTUS DOES HIS BIT: A True-to-Life Farce—ANNAJANSKA, the Bolshevik Empress: A Revolutionary Romancelet.

WORKS BY THE SAME AUTHOR—*continued.*

DRAMATIC WORKS—*continued.*

PLAYS, PLEASANT AND UNPLEASANT. 2 vols. With a Portrait of the Author by FREDERICK H. EVANS, and the original Prefaces. 7s. 6d. net each. Sold separately. VOL. I. UNPLEASANT. (1) Widowers' Houses; (2) The Philanderer; (3) Mrs. Warren's Profession. VOL. II. PLEASANT. (4) Arms and the Man; (5) Candida; (6) The Man of Destiny; (7) You Never Can Tell.

THREE PLAYS FOR PURITANS. 1 vol. 7s. 6d. net.

PREFACE. Why for Puritans? On Diabolonian Ethics. Better than Shakespear?
8. THE DEVIL'S DISCIPLE, with Photogravure Portrait of General Burgoyne. In Three Acts.
9. CÆSAR AND CLEOPATRA, with Photogravure of Julius Cæsar. In Five Acts.
10. CAPTAIN BRASSBOUND'S CONVERSION. In Three Acts.

MAN AND SUPERMAN, A COMEDY AND A PHILOSOPHY. 1 vol. 7s. 6d. net.

Epistle Dedicatory to ARTHUR BINGHAM WALKLEY.
12. MAN AND SUPERMAN. In Four Acts.
    The Revolutionist's Handbook.
    Maxims for Revolutionists.

ANDROCLES AND THE LION, OVERRULED, PYGMALION. Three Plays. With Prefaces on the Prospects of Christianity, Monogamy, and Phonetics. 1 vol. 7s. 6d. net.

JOHN BULL'S OTHER ISLAND AND MAJOR BARBARA. With Prefaces on Home Rule in Ireland and Egypt and on Christianity and Anarchism. Including also How HE LIED TO HER HUSBAND, a play in One Act with Preface. Three Plays. 1 vol. 7s. 6d. net.

PRESS CUTTINGS (1909). A Topical Sketch. Paper, 2s. net.

DRAMATIC WORKS—*continued.*

THE DOCTOR'S DILEMMA, GETTING MARRIED, AND THE SHEWING-UP OF BLANCO POSNET. Three Plays. With Prefaces on the Medical Profession, on Marriage, and on the Censorship. 1 vol. 7s. 6d. net.

MISALLIANCE, THE DARK LADY OF THE SONNETS, AND FANNY'S FIRST PLAY. Three Plays. With Prefaces on Parents and Children and on Shakespear. 1 vol. 7s. 6d. net.

Separate editions of most of the Plays in Paper, 2s., in Cloth, 3s. net each. How He Lied to Her Husband and The Admirable Bashville are in one volume. Overruled and The Dark Lady of the Sonnets are also in one volume.

ESSAYS IN PHILOSOPHIC CRITICISM.

THE QUINTESSENCE OF IBSENISM. Third Edition, 1922. A Completion of the first (1891) edition. 5s. net.

THE PERFECT WAGNERITE. Fourth Edition, 1923. 5s. net.

DRAMATIC OPINIONS AND ESSAYS. Originally contributed to *The Saturday Review* in 1895-98. Selected by JAMES HUNEKER, with a Preface by him. 2 vols. 24s.

THE SANITY OF ART. A reply to Dr. Max Nordau's DEGENERATION. Originally contributed to *Liberty* in 1895. Reprinted with a Preface 1908.
[*New Edition in Preparation.*]

WORKS BY THE SAME AUTHOR—*continued.*

POLITICAL AND ECONOMIC.

FABIAN ESSAYS, 1889. By BERNARD SHAW, SIDNEY WEBB, WILLIAM CLARKE, SYDNEY OLIVIER, C.M.G., Mrs. ANNIE BESANT, and HUBERT BLAND. *Popular Edition, in Paper, 2s. 6d., Cloth, 4s.*

FABIANISM AND THE FISCAL QUESTION, 1904. 1s. net.

FABIAN TRACTS (Various), 1d. or 2d. Apply to the Secretary, Fabian Society, 25 Tothill Street, Westminster, London, S.W.

THE COMMON SENSE OF MUNICIPAL TRADING, 1904. Reprinted 1908 and 1922. 1s. 6d. net.

HOW TO SETTLE THE IRISH QUESTION, 1917. 6d.

PEACE CONFERENCE HINTS, 1919. Cr. 8vo. 1s. 6d. net.

SELECTIONS.

SELECTED PASSAGES FROM THE WORKS OF BERNARD SHAW. Chosen by CHARLOTTE F. SHAW. With a photogravure of the bust of Bernard Shaw by Rodin. *New popular edition.* The selections are drawn from all the works published up to 1914, and to some extent from unpublished correspondence.